MAIDS&MISTRESSES

Celebrating 300 years of Women and the Yorkshire Country House

Edited by Ruth M. Larsen

YCHP
YORKSHIRE
COUNTRY HOUSE
PARTNERSHIP

MAIDS&MISTRESSES

Published by The Yorkshire Country House Partnership,
Castle Howard, York, YO60 7DA

ISBN 0-9547516-0-4

Designed by Stubbs Design, Ilkley

Typeset in Clarendon and Bembo

Printed by Henry Ling Limited, Dorchester

Contents

Foreword

The Yorkshire Country House Partnership was formed in 1999 when the University of York and seven of the houses in the region (Brodsworth Hall, Burton Constable, Castle Howard, Harewood House, Lotherton Hall, Nostell Priory and Temple Newsam) established a programme of inter-disciplinary research into the history, families, collections, archives and estates connected with these great houses.

The establishment of the Partnership marked a special opportunity for scholars from the Departments of History, Archaeology, Art History, and the Centre for Eighteenth Century Studies to pursue collaborative research with the curators from these houses, which would lead to publications, exhibitions, and conferences that would open up the histories of these houses to broader audiences, both academic and non-specialist.

Among the many possible subjects for research identified in the early stages of the Partnership, that of Women and the Yorkshire Country House took shape most immediately. Much of this topic has been defined by the postgraduate work of Dr Ruth Larsen, whose research has been invaluable in casting light on the role played by women in some of these houses. A programme of seminars and a day conference, held during 2000-2001, also allowed the curators in individual houses to advance their own understanding of the subject.

The programme of seven simultaneous exhibitions, entitled *Maids & Mistresses*, held in the seven houses during 2004, and generously supported by the Heritage Lottery Fund under the 'Your Heritage' scheme, has enabled the houses to display these findings to the visiting public. The concept of interlinked exhibitions, forming an 'exhibition itinerary', represents an untested format in the tradition of country house displays. By presenting the wealth of new material in situ in each of the houses across the region, important connections and points of comparison have opened up between the histories of these houses, and thereby enabled a deeper understanding of the subject to emerge.

An international conference, hosted jointly by the University of York and Castle Howard in May 2004, has encouraged scholars from different disciplines to contribute to the debate on the role women have played in the British country house.

Exhibitions, conferences, and related events are by their very nature ephemeral. While many of the objects within the collections of these great houses will remain on permanent display, the specific focus established for the year, namely to represent the country house through the lives and achievements of its female occupants, will be replaced by other perspectives in years to come. The Partnership therefore wished to mark the culmination of this project with a publication that would draw together research into various aspects of each house, together with an overview of the subject.

It is intended that this volume should mark the first in a series of Yorkshire Country House Partnership publications, with future titles focusing on other projects as and when they reach fruition. Further information on the research activities of the Partnership can be found at www.ychp.org.uk

Christopher Ridgway and Allen Warren
Co-Chairs Yorkshire Country House Partnership

ACKNOWLEDGEMENTS

Many individuals have assisted the editor and the contributors, generously offering advice and the benefit of their knowledge, and our thanks extend to the archivists and librarians whose cooperation has enabled many hidden stories to be uncovered. We are grateful to the University of York, especially Dr Allen Warren and Dr Jane Rendall of the Department of History, who were instrumental in the formation of the Yorkshire Country House Partnership, and who have actively encouraged the study of the women of the country houses in the region. In addition we are grateful to the owners, administrators and other staff attached to the houses for their encouragement and assistance; and for making available material from their collections. We are especially indebted to Alison Brisby, Jean Hunter, Terry Suthers, Professor W. M. Ormrod, Bill Connor and Rosemary Evans for their help in the project. Our thanks also go to Den Stubbs for his work on the design of this volume, as well as the related exhibitions.

We would like to express our gratitude to the Marc Fitch fund, and the Leeds Art Collections Fund for their financial assistance towards this volume. We are also grateful to Sue Final from the Research and Industry Office at the University of York, who supported the project during its early stages by funding the appointment of a project coordinator, Jocelyn Friel; her assessment of the planning for the exhibitions was invaluable in determining how the project should come to fruition.

Finally, none of this would have been possible without the Heritage Lottery Fund, whose generous support for the inter-linked exhibitions, through the 'Your Heritage' grant scheme, has enabled the lives of the Maids and Mistresses of Yorkshire's great country houses to be understood and appreciated by everyone.

Introduction:
'Secret Springs' – Unlocking the Histories of the Women of the Yorkshire Country House

RUTH M. LARSEN

I n her advice manual *Thoughts in the Form of Maxims Addressed to Young Ladies on Their First Establishment in the World*, Isabella Carlisle encouraged young women to hide the tools that ensured the smooth running of a country house. Her advice encapsulates the problems that the scholar faces when exploring the women associated with these buildings. The women of both upstairs and downstairs appear to have been so good at concealing how they managed the large establishments that even the more determined spectator can find it difficult to discover what it was they did in the buildings. Modern visitors to country houses have also found the 'secret springs' to be hidden. The houses appear to be museums, fancy structures that display the art of male collectors, not the homes of important women of the past, who appear only as beauties on the wall. While, in some instances, laundries, kitchens and other service areas have recently been opened to the public, the nature of the lives of both the servants and chatelaines who inhabited them have been largely ignored.

However, some of the great country houses of Yorkshire are beginning to change this perception. During 2004, a series of exhibitions were launched to explore the role that women played in these buildings, uncovering both their private lives and their public personas. These took place in seven houses across the county: Brodsworth Hall, Burton Constable, Castle Howard, Harewood House, Lotherton Hall, Nostell Priory, and Temple Newsam. The exhibitions and this associated publication aim to demonstrate that the country house was, and is, a place where women played an active and important role. By exploring their writings, studying their oral testimonies, and considering their portraits, and other sources, it has been possible to uncover the nature of the lifestyles of these women. Their roles and responsibilities have emerged, as well as their dreams and disappointments, their hopes and fears. It is now possible to share these stories, and to unlock the history of the maids and mistresses of the Yorkshire country house.

The image of the elite woman of the country houses has been subject to satire, invention and misunderstanding. Eighteenth-century commentators, such as Mary

Conceal, from the indifferent spectator, the secret springs which move, regulate and perfect the arrangement of your household.

Isabella, Dowager Countess of Carlisle, 1789. [1]

Wollstonecraft, criticised and attacked wealthy and fashionable women, and these assessments have continued to have currency in the work of twentieth-century historians. She wrote in 1792: 'Women in particular all want to be ladies, which is simply to have nothing to do, but listlessly to go they scarcely care where for they cannot tell what.'[2] Elite women were condemned for lacking utility and enjoying indolent, uneducated, and selfish lifestyles. During the seventeenth century, the negative stereotype of the wealthy wife was: 'the idle city dame, ever gadding, ever gossiping and tattling'.[3] Aristocratic women were criticised for being virulent consumers, and the purchase of luxury goods was seen as a particularly female activity, which demonstrated a lack of both sensibility and prudence. Numerous commentators criticised female enjoyment of both shopping and visiting; these were described as time-wasting hobbies which had little purpose and were only for show.[4] In the section of his *History of Women* (1779) that explored 'Amusements and methods of killing time', William Alexander noted that the female nature:

constantly shews [sic] a greater proclivity to the gay and the amusive, than to the sober and useful scenes of life; and loves better to sport away time amid the flowers that strow [sic] the path of pleasure, than to be entangled among the briars and thorns which perplex the path of care.[5]

This disposition for display and performance among fashionable women was a central feature of many of the criticisms levelled against them. They were presented as being essentially deceitful, and trying to hide their true natures. The purchasing and use of makeup by women was criticised by Jonathan Swift in his poem 'The Lady's Dressing Room' (1732), where the dressing table was described as laden thus:

Here gallpots and vials placed,
Some filled with washes, some with paste,
Some with pomatum, paints and slops,
And ointments good for scabby chops.[6]

Swift's poem not only described, with great disgust, what lay underneath the facade of fashionable beauty, but also how men were duped by the oils and ointments, bewitched and unable to see the real woman. The falseness of elites was of particular concern during the eighteenth century, heightened by the popularity of the masquerade. This newly popular form of entertainment was criticised for creating moral disorder, as people could pretend to be what they were not.[7]

The reasons why aristocratic women faced such attacks on their character are numerous. Some writers were provoked by their concerns about female influence on political society, and therefore on how the country was run. In the late seventeenth-century the authority of Court women was questioned; female power was considered to be uncontrolled and irrational. Some contemporaries thought that women such as Sarah, Duchess of Marlborough threatened the social order, and so criticised them by exaggerating their power. In the later eighteenth century, Georgiana, fifth Duchess of Devonshire, was also criticised for her political influence, although this was in relation to the constituency of Westminster rather than the Court. In 1784 she publicly canvassed for votes for Charles Fox. While it was normal practice for elite women to support the campaigns of their fathers, husbands and brothers, it was unusual for a woman to actively support a man who was not a relative. This was seen as unacceptable behaviour by Fox's opposition, and so they encouraged the Tory press to rebuke Georgiana and her campaign, and used satirical prints that questioned her femininity and chastity.[8]

Attacks on elite women, however, were not confined to a few famous politically active women. Most commentators presented fashionable women as lazy and self-obsessed instead. Many writers from the 1650s through to the twentieth century have portrayed aristocratic women as guilty of being idle and uncaring, and lacking the very virtues essential for them to be successful mothers and wives. In 'The Rape of the Lock' (1714) Alexander Pope ridiculed a fashionable woman's inability to rouse herself from sleep, and then enduring an empty and aimless day.[9] By the nineteenth century, the image of the elite woman was that of a selfish social butterfly, who might play 'Lady Bountiful' for her own benefit, but who really cared little for anything other than herself and her frivolous social circle. Didactic literature ridiculed the image of the elite woman in order to hold 'Folly to the light', as was Addison's aim in his writings in *The Spectator* magazine.[10] In the mid-nineteenth century, upper-class women faced attack by those who were against the elite political system of the time, and so were critical of both male and female aristocrats. These detractors used the image of the childlike, decorative, feminine elite woman to undermine the authority and agency of all of those in government.[11] The majority of these portrayals of women were polemical, used to forward the arguments of those wishing to encourage women of all social classes to become domestically-minded and morally engaged individuals.

The rhetoric of these attacks has continued to have an impact, and has been used by twentieth-century historians to describe the actual behaviour of elite women. Often presented by historians as a homogeneous mass of 'identikit' women, their image has often been based on the polemical ideas of the period rather than modern research (fig. 1). This book challenges this approach, and uses the writings of the women of the past to explore their lives in the country houses of Yorkshire. It considers both elite women and servants, and presents a more measured view of their histories. Recent studies have led to a growing awareness of the diversity of experiences that country house women enjoyed. Historians such as Elaine Chalus and Kim Reynolds have examined the important role that elite women played in political society, and their ability to become public figures, within certain constraints.[12] Some have looked at how they shaped and decorated their houses, and the role they played in creating the country house.[13] However, there have been few systematic surveys of the domestic experiences of the women living in country houses. Amanda Vickery's work has provided a major contribution to modern understandings of this area, although not exclusively concerned with women associated with great country houses. *The Gentleman's Daughter* examines the lives of a group of genteel women primarily, though not exclusively, based in Lancashire.[14] It is especially concerned with their family life, relations between a mistress and her servants, social networks, and consumption patterns, exploring the

FIGURE 1
The Three Howard Daughters, by Antonio Pellegrini, c. 1712, oil on canvas.
THE CASTLE HOWARD COLLECTION

Although the sisters were aged between eleven and seventeen years old at the time the painting was produced, their youth and the diversity of their ages is not represented in the image; instead they have been presented as interchangeable young women.

ways in which goods conferred politeness, domesticity and elegance. The specific role of wife and mother is considered in Judith Lewis' examination of childbearing among the aristocracy in the later eighteenth and nineteenth centuries.[15] Through a survey of physical and emotional issues regarding the birth of children she found evidence of a growing affection within aristocratic families in the nineteenth century, and her work highlights the possibilities for understanding familial dynamics. Jessica Gerard's *Country House Life* uses the building of the elite home as the basis for her study of the family life of the aristocracy for the period 1815-1915.[16] Although not exclusively concerned with female experiences, she studies the role that women played in the domestic lives of the upper classes, and the issues that affected their lives, including relations between parents and children, and courtship and marriage. Like Lewis, she finds evidence of an affectionate and domestic attitude within aristocratic families in the nineteenth century, and demonstrates that detailed information regarding the private and emotional lives of past women exists. These studies have highlighted that with dedicated research, we can gain a much wider and deeper understanding regarding the nature of life in the country house

So what was life like for women in the country houses of Yorkshire? In order to answer this question it is important to recognise that their differing social circumstances, the time period in which they were living, and the nature of their relationships with the other women in the household would have had a major effect on individual's opportunities and experiences. The life of a dowager countess in Temple Newsam at the start of the eighteenth century would have been very different from that of a young servant starting her working life at Brodsworth Hall just before the First World War. However, the research behind the *Maids & Mistresses* exhibitions has shown many similarities and common themes, including the joys and disappointments of marriage, the importance of work and the desire for affection.

The childhood of the elite women of the country house has emerged as often being a happy time, where girls enjoyed a good level of education and parental care. The relationship between Frances, ninth Viscountess Irwin of Temple Newsam and her five daughters in the mid-eighteenth century reflects this idea. She and her husband did not have any sons, which led to the loss of the family's title. Although Frances recognised the importance of a son and heir, and called it her 'one thing needful', she did not love her daughters any less because of their gender.[17] She wrote about her motherly pride throughout her life, and the daughters were celebrated in an animated portrait by Benjamin Wilson, which shows them at play in pink dresses, highlighting both their youthfulness and their femininity (cover illustration). Studies have shown that by, at least, the late eighteenth century, daughters were cherished, especially by their mothers. They were often placed into the supervision of their mother rather than a nurse, who would care for them and be responsible for teaching them basic education skills before a tutor was hired. As they spent so much time with them and shared many activities, women began to favour the companionship of daughters, and

FIGURE 2
Mrs Scott and her daughter Henrietta, by Richard Cosway, oil on canvas.

Paintings portraying the affectionate relationship between mothers and daughters were increasingly popular from the later eighteenth century onwards.

lamented the lack of female children as others had previously mourned an absence of sons (fig. 2).[18]

A great deal of investment was placed into a daughter's education. They were not only taught reading, writing and arithmetic, but also foreign languages, history, classical literature. These academic skills were balanced with training in the accomplishments: dancing, music, drawing and needlework. Most young women were educated at home, normally by a governess or a tutor. The nature of their home education can be discovered through records kept by the young women, such as the exercise book kept by thirteen-year-old Aline Thellusson, who lived in Brodsworth Hall in the 1860s.[19] Georgiana Cavendish, later sixth countess of Carlisle, of Castle Howard, also kept a school register book (fig. 3).[20] This details the lessons and educational experiences that she encountered as a fifteen-year-old girl growing up at Chatsworth. She made a daily log during 1798 of the tasks she undertook, placing them under headings such as 'music', 'reading', 'drawing', and 'company and conversation'. Both Aline and Georgiana studied religious texts, and moral values played an important role in female education in this time period. However, they were also taught the traditional accomplishments, and these were skills that many of the women in this survey continued to value into their adulthood. While it was usual for sons to be sent away to school, this was less common among daughters, unless there was a specific need. As Catholics, the Constable family sent their daughters either to the Bar Convent School at York, or to be educated in France, in order that they could guarantee that the needs of their faith were met in their educational programme. For those parents who wanted to educate their children at home, the hiring of staff could be costly. Those who could afford it would bring in an army of specialist tutors, such as drawing masters and language specialists, in order to complement the permanent tutor's skills. Even for those who were educated at home, a great deal of money could be invested into their education: it was not necessarily a sign of academic neglect to educate a daughter within the country house.

The skills that young women learnt in their childhood were often designed with the ultimate aim of marriage in mind. The accomplishments would make young woman attractive and appear genteel, as well as preparing them for married life. Young women were often well-educated in the classics and history, and so would be able to converse with future husbands, and support them in forming networks with other families and individuals. From the early eighteenth century onwards there was an increasing emphasis on marriages based on mutual affection and companionship, where the couple would seek a form of partnership both emotionally and practically. Although some aristocratic women were forced into arranged marriages, the majority had some control over who would be their future spouse. Assemblies, balls and private parties would mean that elites could socialise with other suitable young people. London's marriage market was securely managed so that young sons and daughters could be given the freedom to marry who they liked, as long as the only people they met were those that attended the parties. Clubs such as Almack's allowed only the 'socially fit' to become members and buy

FIGURE 3
Georgiana, sixth Countess of Carlisle, with her daughters Caroline and Harriet, by John Jackson, c. 1810, oil on canvas.
THE CASTLE HOWARD COLLECTION

tickets for their balls and suppers, therefore enforcing a strict social hierarchy by only allowing the most fashionable to enter the aristocratic world. This meant that it was not necessary for parents to arrange marriages; instead they could engineer the social world so that their children would find someone suitable, but of their own choosing.

The 'market' did not always work, though, leading to some women having to fight to marry the husband of their choice. In the mid-eighteenth century, for example, Frances Shepherd, a rich heiress, was forbidden from marrying a peer in the will of her father. However, so determined was she to wed Charles Ingram, heir to Temple Newsam and the title of Viscount Irwin, that she had to arrange for a private bill to be brought to Parliament, so that she could marry in spite of restrictions in the will. She was successful, and enjoyed a long and happy marriage, and her letters to her friends are full of declarations of her love for her husband, even after many years together.[21] Other matches were less suitable in terms of a match of social class. Esther Winn of Nostell Priory flouted the rules of the class system and the authority of her mother, by eloping with the family baker in 1792.[22] A few years later Edward, Viscount Lascelles, the eldest son of the second Earl of Harewood was disinherited after his marriage to his mistress.[23] It was not only the upper classes who could lose their home and income through marriage. As the essay on Brodsworth Hall explores, female servants were expected to give up work once they married, therefore leaving the house where they may have lived for many years.

That people were willing to give up a great deal in order to get married indicates that many believed that a loving companion could bring them happiness. There were a great deal of happy marriages within the families included within this volume, and the love letters between some couples are still heart warming today. In the later eighteenth century the fifth Earl of Carlisle wrote to his wife: 'I love you to a degree that few, very few, can understand, and to own the truth, more that I myself had any ideas of', The collection of letters between this couple reflect the very deep affection that could exist between husbands and wives.[24] However, while a happy marriage was an ideal that most women of all social classes sought, it was not always an obtainable dream. Not all marriages were contented, as the cases of Isabella Countess of Carlisle and Lady Dorothy Seymour Worsley illustrate (plates 12 and 13).[25] Other women decided not to get married. Marriage could reduce a woman's freedom to follow her own interests and desires. Elite single women were often active philanthropists, as was the case with the Gascoigne sisters of Lotherton Hall.[26] Marriage could also limit one's ability to follow a career, either in service in a country houses for women of the lower orders, or as an active member of the Royal Household for the daughters of the elites. During the eighteenth century nearly a quarter of aristocratic women did not marry, indicating that marriage was not seen as the only route to happiness available to the women of the country house (fig. 4).[27]

The importance of work is another theme that has emerged through the studies of the women in these houses. The labour of female servants was crucial to the

FIGURE 4

William and Winifred Constable in Rome as Cato and Marcia, by Anton Maron, 1773, oil on canvas.
BURTON CONSTABLE HALL

Winifred did not marry, and instead supported her brother in the running of Burton Constable.

running of the establishments; they really were the 'secret springs', shadowy figures who the visitors to the buildings were not supposed to see.[28] Most of them were engaged in labour intensive cleaning, cooking and laundry, and so would not have normally developed any form of relationship with the family (fig. 5). Others, though, worked much more closely with their employers. The housekeeper may have had regular meetings with the mistress in order to discuss the management of staff, household expenses and other issues. The housekeeper often acted as a public face of the country house too, showing polite visitors around the properties. Other servants who may have had closer interactions with the family included governesses, companions and lady's maids. Occasionally these could lead to an affectionate relationship. Nanny Dowler, the nurse at Burton Constable, was so favoured among the Constables that at her death she was interred in the mausoleum at Halsham East Yorkshire, which was otherwise reserved only for family. Later in the nineteenth century the companion of the Thellusson girls at Brodsworth Hall married one of the family, Peter Thellusson, the heir to the house. However, while it is clear that the mistresses of the country house were often reliant on their staff, examples of this degree of fondness were rare. Some women, such as Sabine Winn at Nostell Priory, found servants an inconvenience and a source of many troubles. While favoured staff may have been remembered in wills and given cast-off clothing, generally the relationship was one shaped by necessity rather then affection.

It was not only the servants who worked in these houses; the elite women also fulfilled many roles which today would be considered as 'work'. Far from being women who could be described as 'idle drones', they led active lives.[29] Many women took an active interest in the running of their households, most notably Isabella, third Viscountess Irwin at Temple Newsam, whose pocket books offer a fascinating insight into the role that a widowed chatelaine played in managing a country house at the start of the eighteenth century.[30] Some aristocrats were famed for their domestic knowledge; it is interesting that the newly married Howard sisters who grew up at Castle Howard at the start of the nineteenth century were keen to garner advice from Louisa, Countess of Harewood on a range of familial concerns. She was not only good at providing information regarding tutors or curtains, but was also instrumental in redesigning the house in the nineteenth century. Her portrait by George Richmond, c. 1855, (plate 16) portrays her in front of the new terrace that she helped to create. While she is depicted in a distinctly matriarchal fashion, wearing a shawl, the jewels and hair decoration underline her status as an elite woman. She was happy to be depicted as an aristocratic 'domestic goddess'.[31]

Other women were involved in work outside of their home. Much of this was charitable in nature; during the nineteenth century the Gascoigne sisters were active philanthropists, erecting almshouses and churches near Lotherton Hall. In 1937 Adeline Thellusson of Brodsworth Hall was awarded an OBE after many years as matron at St Dunstan's Home for Blind Soldiers in Brighton.[32] Others were more concerned with politics, actively maintaining the family interest in

FIGURE 5
An unidentified still-room maid.
BRODSWORTH HALL

Westminster. Frances, ninth Viscountess Irwin became embroiled in a bitter dispute with the Duke of Norfolk over the parliamentary seat of Horsham, which the Temple Newsam family had controlled throughout the eighteenth century.[33] Others worked for the Royal Court; Lady Anne Irwin (née Howard), her niece Anne Howard and Emma Lady Portman (née Lascelles) all held positions in the Royal Household, which gave them and their families considerable influence. Harriet Howard, who lived at Castle Howard until her marriage to the second Duke of Sutherland, became Mistress of the Robes to Queen Victoria. This role gave her considerable status. She not only had the chance to influence the monarch, who appears to have had high regard for Harriet's opinions, but her position also offered her a platform from which she could become a society hostess and follow concerns close to her own heart. She invited Garibaldi to her London home, and she was active in the movement to abolish slavery in America, supporting Harriet Beecher-Stowe in her campaign.[34] Of all the women in this survey, the one who had the closest relationship to the Court was, of course, Princess Mary, the wife of the sixth Earl of Harewood (fig. 6). As the Princess Royal she undertook official duties both at home and abroad. Through their work, women of the country houses could have a considerable effect on the world around them, both near and far.

Not all women, though, were this active, and many lived quiet lives dedicated to their families, their homes, and to fulfilling their duties and interests. The essays within this book highlight the great variety of experiences that the different maids and mistresses of the houses enjoyed. Much of the archival material that has been used in researching this project has not been examined in any detail by other scholars, and the information that they contain has not been brought out into the public arena before now. The studies show that the life of the country house woman is not easily categorised, but can encompass a wide range of opportunities, restrictions and disappointments.

Caroline Carr-Whitworth and Virginia Arrowsmith highlight this variety most starkly by comparing the experiences of the owners of the house, Brodsworth Hall, to those endured by their servants. Although the house has only limited archival material relating to its women, it has been possible to draw out important information regarding female attitudes towards marriage, motherhood, leisure and work, among other topics. These themes have been illuminated by oral history recordings, a collection of testimonies given by former servants of the property. Through these we can gain an important insight into their thoughts regarding the house, their work, and their employers. While the different social backgrounds of the women associated with Brodsworth had a considerable impact in shaping their experiences, there are a number of similarities between the maids and the mistresses. For example, both groups were educated with a clear understanding of their future role, whether it was to be an accomplished lady or a lady's maid. Motherhood offered women some degree of security in the future, and producing heirs who would care for them in their old age was a concern for women of all social classes. Both groups of women were committed to doing what they

FIGURE 6
HRH Princess Mary,
the Princess Royal.
THE EARL AND COUNTESS OF HAREWOOD
AND THE TRUSTEES OF THE HAREWOOD
HOUSE TRUST

perceived as being best for themselves and for their families, a pattern which can be detected in many of the lives explored in this volume.

Both Gerardine M. Mulcahy and Christopher Ridgway explore the struggles of two women to fulfil the roles which society, and life, ascribed to them. The story of Lady Chichester, of Burton Constable and her role as an officer's wife reflects the wide range of experiences that faced elite women in the nineteenth century. She had a loving husband whose position meant that she had to spend a great deal of time away from him. She cared deeply for her children, but, unfortunately, this did not limit the risk of untimely deaths. As the essay highlights, not all country house women lived a life closely tied to the home, but some travelled a great deal, especially in Europe. While it is clear that Mary Barbara fulfilled many of the ideals of the dedicated wife and mother, it is more difficult to assess the behaviour of Isabella, fourth Countess of Carlisle, of Castle Howard, who was also no stranger to travelling across the Continent. Christopher Ridgway presents the life of the great aunt of the poet, Lord Byron, as being far more complex than previously supposed. Isabella has often been seen as a 'scandalous' woman of the type much derided by Mary Wollstonecraft. However, by examining the fuller context of her story, one can identify a rounded figure, who had more in common with both Wollstonecraft and Lady Chichester than first appears.

Women who reflect both ends of the spectrum regarding ideals of female behaviour feature in Karen Lynch's exploration of the Lascelles ladies of Harewood House. From the domestic oracle of Louisa, third Countess, to the scandal prone Lady Worsley, this essay demonstrates how the nature of life for the women associated with the country house cannot be easily defined. By taking a chronological approach, this survey highlights the important role that the women played in the history of the house. Wives, daughters, sisters and cousins were crucial in forming networks with other families and individuals, representing the family in the Court and wider society, and ensuring, or damaging, familial reputation. Women were central in shaping the successes of the Lascelles dynasty over the last three hundred years, and in promoting and maintaining the family's status.

Adam White also explores the lives of women who were active in maintaining the family interest in their estate. Mary Isabella and Elizabeth Gascoigne of Lotherton Hall played an active role in managing the land and properties in both Yorkshire and Ireland that they had inherited in 1843. The essay explores their role in managing the income from their estate, their philanthropic activities, and their recreations and pastimes. What is presented is a detailed study of sisterhood in the nineteenth century, and the benefits that such a partnership offered young elite women. Their success in maintaining the estate indicates the important role that unmarried women could play in shaping the country house and its environs.

The examination of three women associated with Nostell Priory by Christopher Todd and Sophie Raikes also considers the importance of the action of women in shaping the family reputation. When Sabine-Louise d'Hervart, a widowed Swiss lady, married into the Winn family in 1761 there was great concern regarding the impact that having a foreign mistress would have on the name and standing of the family. However, it was her daughter Esther, who eloped with the family baker, who threatened the image of the family and its dynastic future most of all. As the essay highlights, though, transgressing one's social class did not necessarily mean that one's children were excluded from a position within elite society.

In the final essay, James Lomax brings together many of these themes by investigating the lives of three women central to the history of Temple Newsam: Isabella and Frances, Viscountesses Irwin, and Emily Meynell Ingram. These women were crucial to the continuation of the relationship between the Ingrams and the house, and each left her own considerable mark on the history of the family. Their roles as wives, mothers, chatelaines, philanthropists, and political managers reflect the great variety of duties and responsibilities that elite women were expected to fulfil. Although they faced personal sorrows, including the deaths of their spouses and children, they managed to work hard to ensure the future of Temple Newsam.

Together, these essays demonstrate the great variety of experiences enjoyed by the women of the country houses of Yorkshire. Many of the elite women had happy marriages, were loving and caring mothers, and played an active role in the local communities. Other women did not fulfil these ideals, and faced difficulties, and even public censure, because of unfortunate decisions or misfortune. As is the case in the modern world, chance and circumstance had a significant effect on the lives of these women; accidents of birth and death shaped the opportunities faced by those of all social classes. However, a number of central themes run through the essays. Many describe affectionate relationships within families, between husbands, wives, sisters, and children; the popular stereotype of arranged and unloving marriages leading to a loveless family life appears to describe the unusual rather than the norm. The majority of elite women were centrally concerned with their domestic world, and were not the scandalous, lazy and frivolous women described by the writers of the eighteenth and nineteenth centuries. A great many of these women were 'fighters' too, willing to contemplate difficult circumstances to be with their loved ones, to live the lifestyle of their choosing, and to maintain the status of the family. The women of both upstairs and downstairs were dedicated to ensuring the future success of the country houses and their families. Their stories reflect the lives of women who were acutely aware of their roles and responsibilities, and who lived active and largely fulfilled lives. Women were central figures in the country houses of Yorkshire, and it is only by uncovering their lives that we can gain a richer, fuller, truer understanding of these remarkable buildings and their inhabitants.

The Department of History at the University of York and the Arts and Humanities Research Board financially supported the research which forms the basis of this introduction, for which I acknowledge my gratitude.

1   Carlisle, I., *Thoughts in the Form of Maxims Addressed to Young Ladies on Their First Establishment in the World* (London, 1789), p. 32.

2   Wollstonecraft, M., *A Vindication of the Rights of Woman* (Oxford, 1993), p. 229.

3   Mendelson, S.H., and P. Crawford, *Women in Early Modern England, 1550-1720* (Oxford, 1998), p. 67.

4   See Guest, H., *Small Change. Women, Learning, Patriotism, 1750-1810* (Chicago, Ill., 2000), pp. 70-98.

5   Alexander, W., *The History of Women, From the Earliest Antiquity, to the Present Time; Giving Some Account of Almost Every Interesting Particular Concerning That Sex, Among All Nations, Ancient and Modern* (Dublin, 1779), i, p. 105.

6   Swift, J., 'The Lady's Dressing Room', in *Selected Poems*, P. Rogers (ed.), (London, 1993), pp. 129-33, lines 33-6.

7   See, for example, Pitt, C., 'On the Masquerades' (1727), in *The New Book of Eighteenth Century Verse*, R. Lonsdale (ed.), (Oxford, 1984), pp. 198-9.

8   A selection of these images appears in Foreman, A., *Georgiana's World. The Illustrated Georgiana, Duchess of Devonshire* (London, 2001), pp. 98-9. For a discussion of the 1784 election see Lewis, J.S., '1784 and all that: aristocratic women and electoral politics', in *Women, Privilege, and Power: British Politics, 1750 to the Present*, A. Vickery (ed.), (Stanford, Calif., 2001), pp. 89-122.

9   Pope, A., 'The Rape of the Lock', Canto I, in *Alexander Pope, Oxford Authors*, P. Rogers (ed.), (Oxford, 1993), pp. 79-83.

10 Rogers, K.M., *The Troublesome Helpmate. A History of Misogyny in Literature* (Seattle, Wash., 1966), p. 167.

11 Reynolds, K.D., *Aristocratic Women and Political Society in Victorian Britain* (Oxford, 1998), p. 13.

12 See, for example: Chalus, E., 'Women in English Political Life, 1754-1790' (DPhil Thesis, University of Oxford, 1997); Reynolds, *Aristocratic Women*; Lewis, J.S., *Sacred to Female Patriotism* (London, 2003).

13 Baird, R., *Mistress of the House: Great Ladies and Grand Houses 1670-1830* (London, 2003); Flanders, J., *The Victorian House: Domestic Life from Childbirth to Deathbed* (London, 2003); Lummis, T., and J. Marsh, *The Woman's Domain: Women and the English Country House* (London, 1993).

14 Vickery, A., *The Gentleman's Daughter. Women's Lives in Georgian England* (London, 1998).

15 Lewis, J.S., *In the Family Way. Childbearing in the British Aristocracy 1760-1860* (New Brunswick, N.J., 1986).

16 Gerard, J., *Country House Life, Family and Servants, 1815-1914* (Oxford, 1994).

17 PRO 30/29/4/2/4, Frances Shepheard to Susan Stewart, Temple Newsam, 10 February 1763.

18 Lewis, *In the Family Way*, p. 65.

19 See Arrowsmith and Carr-Whitworth, 'Emerging from the Shadows', this volume.

20 Carlisle MSS, J18/62/2, Register Book.

21 See Lomax, 'Temple Newsam', this volume, and Larsen, R.M., 'Dynastic Domesticity: The Role of Elite Women in the Yorkshire Country House, 1685-1858' (PhD Thesis, University of York, 2003), pp. 133-6.

22 See Todd and Raikes, 'Love, Rebellion and Redemption', this volume.

23 See Lynch, 'Lascelles Ladies', this volume.

24 For example: Carlisle MSS, J15/1/2-6, Frederick fifth Earl of Carlisle to Caroline Carlisle.

25 See Ridgway, 'Isabella, fourth Countess of Carlisle', and Lynch, 'Lascelles Ladies', this volume.

26 See White, 'Mary Isabella and Elizabeth Gascoigne', this volume.

27 Hollingsworth, T.H., 'Demography of the British Peerage', Supplement to *Population Studies* 18.2 (1964), p. 20. For a discussion of the experiences of elite single women see Larsen, 'Dynastic Domesticity', pp. 188-200.

28 For surveys of the role of country house servants see: Christie, C., *The British Country House in the Eighteenth Century* (Manchester, 2000); Gerard, *Country House Life*; Horn, P., *The Rise and Fall of the Victorian Servant* (Dublin, 1975); Sambrook, P., *The Country House Servant* (Stroud, 1999); Waterson, M., *The Servants' Hall, A Domestic History* (London, 1980).

29 Lawrence Stone uses the term 'idle drones' to describe upper-class women in his *Family, Sex and Marriage in England 1500-1800* (London, 1977), p. 396.

30 See Lomax, 'Temple Newsam'.

31 See Lynch, 'Lascelles Ladies'.

32 See Arrowsmith and Carr-Whitworth, 'Emerging from the Shadows', and White, 'Mary Isabella and Elizabeth Gascoigne'.

33 See Lomax, 'Temple Newsam', and Chalus, E., 'Women, electoral privilege and practice in the eighteenth century', in Gleadle, K., and S. Richardson (eds.), *Women in British Politics, 1760-1860: The Power of the Petticoat* (London, 2000), pp. 14-38.

34 Reynolds, *Aristocratic Women*, pp. 112-3, 122-7, 206.

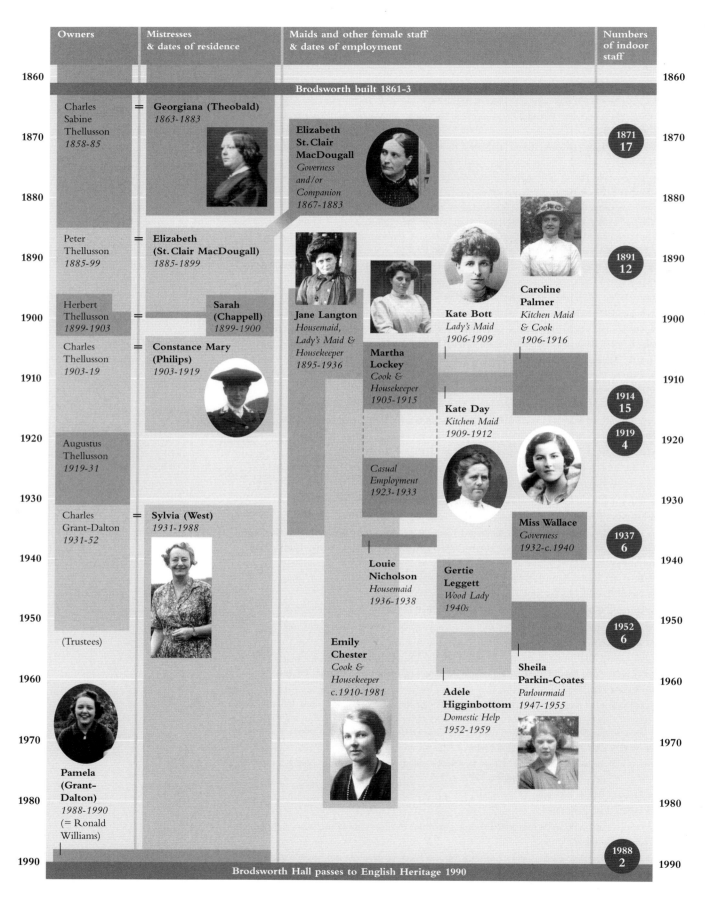

Owners	Mistresses & dates of residence	Maids and other female staff & dates of employment	Numbers of indoor staff

1860

Brodsworth built 1861-3

Charles Sabine Thellusson *1858-85* = **Georgiana (Theobald)** *1863-1883*

1870

Elizabeth St. Clair MacDougall *Governess and/or Companion 1867-1883*

1871 17

1880

Peter Thellusson *1885-99* = **Elizabeth (St. Clair MacDougall)** *1885-1899*

Caroline Palmer *Kitchen Maid & Cook 1906-1916*

1890

1891 12

Herbert Thellusson *1899-1903* = **Sarah (Chappell)** *1899-1900*

Jane Langton *Housemaid, Lady's Maid & Housekeeper 1895-1936*

Kate Bott *Lady's Maid 1906-1909*

1900

Charles Thellusson *1903-19* = **Constance Mary (Philips)** *1903-1919*

Martha Lockey *Cook & Housekeeper 1905-1915*

1910

Kate Day *Kitchen Maid 1909-1912*

1914 15

Augustus Thellusson *1919-31*

1920

Casual Employment 1923-1933

1919 4

1930

Charles Grant-Dalton *1931-52* = **Sylvia (West)** *1931-1988*

Miss Wallace *Governess 1932-c.1940*

1937 6

1940

Louie Nicholson *Housemaid 1936-1938*

Gertie Leggett *Wood Lady 1940s*

1950

1952 6

(Trustees)

Emily Chester *Cook & Housekeeper c.1910-1981*

Sheila Parkin-Coates *Parlourmaid 1947-1955*

1960

Adele Higginbottom *Domestic Help 1952-1959*

1970

Pamela (Grant-Dalton) *1988-1990 (= Ronald Williams)*

1980

Brodsworth Hall passes to English Heritage 1990

1988 2

1990

FIGURE 1

1 2

Emerging from the Shadows: Maids and Mistresses at Brodsworth Hall

VIRGINIA ARROWSMITH & CAROLINE CARR-WHITWORTH

Brodsworth Hall near Doncaster, built in the early 1860s, was the home of the Thellussons and Grant-Daltons until it was given to English Heritage in 1990.[1] Most of the women who lived and worked in the house have until now received little attention, shadows in the male-dominated world which shaped their lives. Their brief appearances in the documentary record belie their contribution to the many and varied aspects of domestic, social and economic life at the Hall. They were an essential part of the country house community, ensuring its efficient day-to-day running and supporting the needs and activities of their respective masters and husbands. The women of both the family and their staff are considered here together, through the different stages of their lives. This gives a fuller picture of the female community at Brodsworth, their interdependent roles and relationships, and the ways in which these changed over time (fig. 1). Parallels and contrasts between them enable us to assess the extent to which they conformed to both contemporary expectations of women, and to our present understanding of life within the English country house.

The main archival holdings relating to Brodsworth Hall reflect the pattern of succession and management of the estate, and afford only glimpses of women's lives.[2] Very few personal records, such as letters or diaries, have survived to illuminate the lives of female members of the family. The experiences of the female staff are also mostly absent from the surviving documentary record, their entire existence intended to be invisible. The housekeepers' account books do however record the intricate daily workings of life 'below stairs'.[3] Photographs, portraits and certain possessions also help to draw the women out from the shadows of the past. Personal insights into the lives of maids and mistresses at Brodsworth are provided by a series of oral history recordings.[4]

Inheritance

The history of the Thellusson family, and in particular the extraordinary 1797 will of the financier Peter Thellusson, reveal significant, but not always successful, efforts to pass property down the male line.[5] Women have been recorded merely as links in the family chain, as wives and providers of male heirs who might qualify for the inheritance. Peter Thellusson, from a Swiss-French family of bankers and merchants, established himself in business in London in 1760. He bought property, including the Brodsworth estate, beginning the rise of the Thellusson family into the ranks of the English landed gentry. His will directed that his property should accumulate over several lifetimes, and eventually be inherited 'by the eldest male lineal descendant of my three sons then living'. After lengthy legal disputes, one half of the inheritance, including the Brodsworth estate, came to Charles Sabine Thellusson in 1858. His wife, Georgiana Theobald, like many women, brought wealth to the family through marriage, which was much needed in the years before he came into his own inheritance.[6] Her fortune was derived from her grandfather's successful hosiery business, and her heirlooms included family and equestrian portraits, many of which still hang at Brodsworth. Using this inheritance, Charles Sabine was swift to demolish the old house and build the present Brodsworth Hall to suit the needs of both his young family and social life, as well as house the staff and activities required to support them.[7]

The Brodsworth estate and Georgiana's property were both passed on through male entail to each of their four sons in turn, their wives Elizabeth, Sarah and Constance Mary becoming successive mistresses of Brodsworth.[8] Sadly, none of these marriages produced children, and so the estate passed through Constance, daughter of Charles and Georgiana, to her son Charles Grant Dalton in 1931. He in turn had no sons and his widow, Sylvia, continued to live at the Hall until her death in 1988. It was their daughter Pamela Williams who decided to pass the house on to English Heritage in 1990, while retaining the estate. Women have thus played an important part in shaping Brodsworth's history.

Representations of women

The women who lived and worked at Brodsworth were surrounded by female images in the form of paintings and sculptures, which reflected complex and conflicting social values and expectations of women. The 1804 Sir Thomas Lawrence portrait of Mrs Thellusson, supporting her son standing on her lap (plate 1), celebrates her achievement in producing an heir. Margaret Carpenter's portrait of Georgiana sitting with a basket of flowers (plate 2) is a vision of placid femininity, painted in 1850, the year of her marriage to Charles Sabine Thellusson. Further female portraits by Nicolas Largillière, Margaret Carpenter and James Ward survive in the house.[9]

The most striking representations of women at Brodsworth are the numerous contemporary Italian sculptures purchased by Charles Sabine Thellusson in 1865.[10] These were displayed prominently throughout the main halls, and also delineate the boundary of the formal garden. While some are copies of classical and neoclassical works, the majority are contemporary designs, and almost all are nude and semi-draped idealised female figures. Thellusson's choice, and perhaps that of

FIGURE 2
Adeline Thellusson in front
of a copy of Venus by
Canova, c. 1907.
ENGLISH HERITAGE

Georgiana too, reflects contrasting ideals of womanhood. *Education* in the Entrance Hall, and *Innocence* and the *Virgin Mary* outside the Drawing Room affirm motherhood, domesticity and purity. However *The Swinging Girl*, *Vanity*, and several *Venuses* present a different view of woman, symbolising pleasure, beauty, love and sexual desire. The contrast between ideals and reality is epitomised by the photograph of Adeline Thellusson in her walking clothes standing in front of a Venus (fig. 2). What the women of Brodsworth thought of these sculptures is not for the most part known, although Sylvia Grant Dalton expressed her generation's distaste for all things Victorian, describing them as 'poor cold ladies' (plate 3).[11] Meanwhile, her housemaid Gladys Phillips (later Jones) expressed mild bemusement at the range of naked female figures which she regularly cleaned until they glistened.[12]

A rich collection of family photographs records women both formally and informally. The amateur photographer Peter Thellusson made haunting studies of his sister Constance and wife Elizabeth in the 1870s-80s. An invaluable group of images taken by another amateur photographer, Alfred Edwards, valet to Charles Thellusson, captures the rare moments of leisure time enjoyed by the staff around 1912-15.[13] Few photographs however record their working lives, underlining the rarity of the image of women in the Brodsworth kitchen from c. 1910 (plate 4).

Education

For maids and mistresses alike, their education was determined both by their sex and social class. This focussed narrowly on providing the skills required for their adult lives. Charles and Georgiana Thellusson followed upper-class tradition in educating their daughters, Aline and Constance, at home and sending their sons away to school, first in Brighton and then to Eton, after their early years together in the nursery. When the family moved into the newly built Brodsworth Hall in 1863, it had day and night nurseries, a schoolroom, and a governess' bedroom.[14] The strong moral and religious content of the girls' education is revealed by a surviving exercise book, from the 1860s, belonging to thirteen-year-old Aline, with questions and answers on Biblical passages.[15] A quiz in its back pages provides fascinating glimpses into female values. Georgiana, as wife, mother, and mistress of the household, declares that Prince Albert is her favourite person, truth her favourite virtue, and 'Peace with everyone' her motto. Answers are also given by Elizabeth St. Clair MacDougall, described as a 'Companion' in 1881, but possibly the governess at this date. She hates 'a hypocrite' and cites 'competency, love and health' as her idea of happiness. Women without independent means, like Elizabeth, often had to rely on their education for their livelihood, which could be insecure. Constance's marriage in 1883 and the deaths of Aline and Georgiana left Elizabeth without a role, but her situation was happily resolved by her marriage later the same year to Peter Thellusson, Brodsworth's heir (fig. 3).

Both Sylvia (née West), in the early years of the twentieth century, and her daughter Pamela Grant-Dalton in the 1920s and 30s also had governesses. Pamela's

FIGURE 3
Elizabeth St Clair MacDougall photographed by Peter Thellusson c. 1875.
ENGLISH HERITAGE

memories of moving on the hands of the clock in the Brodsworth schoolroom suggest that such an education could be both tedious and socially isolating.[16] Its aim was to prepare a girl to be launched into society and find a suitable husband; Pamela's Court Presentation in 1939 demonstrates the continuance of this tradition even as circumstances were changing so rapidly (fig. 4).

For women born into families on the Brodsworth estate, their education was similarly dictated by expectations of a lifetime of domesticity. Economic necessity overshadowed their lives from an early age. The 1870 Education Act brought a dramatic change in stipulating compulsory elementary education. A new

FIGURE 4
Sylvia and Pamela were both presented at Court in March 1939.
ENGLISH HERITAGE

school was provided by the Thellussons, but its comprehensive log books suggest that education was often of secondary importance to either estate or family requirements.[17] Children of both sexes were regularly absent, working with their families in the fields at key times of the agricultural year well into the early twentieth century. The boys often went bush-beating for the Thellussons' shoot while the girls spent much time learning needlework and other skills which would prepare them for a future of skilled domestic economy, whether at home or in service.[18] For some education was curtailed at an early age: Emily Chester was among several girls forced to leave school a year early in 1909 when it became overcrowded, the opening of the Brodsworth Main Colliery having brought many new families to the area. As the daughter of one of the Hall gardeners, she was given work by the Thellussons. Beginning as a 'garden girl', she continued in employment at the hall through to the early 1980s, when failing health after more than sixty years of dutiful service forced her to retire (fig. 5).

Marriage and Motherhood

Marriage was the primary goal of most women, irrespective of class, providing them with a role as wife and mother. It was undertaken both out of social expectation and economic necessity. Women were expected to marry young and choose partners from their own social rank. This meant their choice was often restricted to a narrow social circle: Constance Thellusson married Horace Grant-Dalton, from a land-owning and distantly related family. Sylvia was seventeen when she married Charles Grant-Dalton, a regular visitor to the Wests, in 1916.

For female staff, coming into service also provided them with the opportunity to meet potential husbands; it has been suggested that this was the working-class

FIGURE 5
Emily Chester spent her life in service at Brodsworth Hall, starting before the First World War and finishing shortly before her death in 1983.
ENGLISH HERITAGE

equivalent of 'coming out' into society.[19] Many of the Brodsworth staff conformed to this pattern, finding partners of equivalent status from within the staff hierarchy. Two consecutive cooks, Martha Lockey and Caroline Palmer, married chauffeurs (George Raper and Alfred Edwards) during the First World War, while housemaids Kathleen Fenn, Gladys Phillips and Louie Nicholson, all married gardeners in the 1930s. In all these instances, the women gave up their paid employment on marriage, in order to fulfil the ideal of women as homemakers, now in service to their husbands and families rather than their employers.

Marriage conferred social status, especially for those becoming the mistress of a large household such as Brodsworth. It also offered many women emotional security. Sarah Chappell, whose first marriage had taken place at an early age after she was orphaned, married Herbert Thellusson in 1885 after only a brief period of widowhood. Marriage could also provide some financial independence: Elizabeth received £200 a year as an 'allowance for private expenditure'.[20] Constance Mary enjoyed the annual interest, but not the capital, on the £10,000 settled on her in 1885 by her husband Charles Thellusson (fig. 6).[21] As mistress, she oversaw household expenditure: the housekeepers' account books are addressed to the respective Mrs Thellussons. Women from working families similarly managed their own household accounts, affording them some degree of financial autonomy.

Motherhood for working-class women ensured some security in their later years, family support often providing vital assistance in old age.[22] Bearing children was equally important for landed families, especially as a male heir secured the family succession. Georgiana Thellusson dutifully produced four sons, although their marriages in turn were less fortunate in remaining childless.

Some women did not marry, either through choice or circumstance. Those in domestic service had the opportunity to pursue a fulfilling career, which could bring authority and status, an option not open to those who chose the alternative path of marriage. A life spent in service also afforded them a degree of financial security, enabling them to accumulate substantial savings. Jane Langton came to Brodsworth in 1895 as a housemaid, progressing up the career ladder to become lady's maid and subsequently housekeeper, holding sway over staff at the hall until her death in 1936. Careers for unmarried women of genteel birth were restricted to those activities considered appropriate for ladies, such as teaching and nursing. The sisters Adeline and Molly Thellusson, relations who often stayed with Charles and Constance Mary, both remained spinsters, and became Voluntary Aid Detachment nurses in the First World War. Adeline was later awarded an OBE for many years of distinguished service as matron of St Dunstan's Home for Blind Soldiers in Brighton.[23]

FIGURE 6
Constance Thellusson married Horace Grant-Dalton in 1883. The Brodsworth estate was inherited by their son Charles in 1931 since her brothers' marriages were childless.
ENGLISH HERITAGE

Work and Leisure

The fundamental difference between maids and mistresses was that the lives of the staff were dictated entirely by the needs of their employers. As the last owner of the hall put it, 'the only difference was they had to work, poor souls, and we didn't, but apart from that ...'[24] Her comment encapsulates an unspoken acceptance of the hierarchical structure, in which everyone had their place.

For the lady of the house, leisure was combined with social duty, which could be seen as a type of 'work'. This was part of the long tradition of benevolence and patronage by landowners and their wives towards their estate families, through which they reinforced their social position. It was also an interdependent relationship. Employment 'up at the big house' encouraged strong loyalty to the Thellussons and Grant-Daltons in return: four generations of the Tissington, Taylor and Handley families have been employed at Brodsworth over the last 150 years, a link which continues today.[25]

The Thellusson and Grant-Dalton ladies actively maintained the tradition of 'Lady Bountiful'.[26] While entertainment of the tenantry on a large scale was often undertaken jointly with their husbands, the ladies maintained regular personal contact, building up good-will between the family and estate. A local obituary of Sarah Thellusson in 1900 describes her in predictably glowing terms as 'a ministering angel':

> *On nearly every day, when the weather permitted, she was visiting in the village and the immediate district, and her visits and the sweet oral greetings with which all and sundry were accosted will by no means be the only things that will be missed.*[27]

Brodsworth School's log books also record that Georgiana, her daughters, and subsequent mistresses of the house were regular visitors to the school. Christmas treats for the schoolchildren were given annually from the 1870s. Sylvia Grant-Dalton continued these traditions until the 1980s, taking a personal interest in the children.[28]

The welfare interests and organisational skills of the 'mistresses' were put to good use in their war efforts, providing a degree of shared experience with estate women. Constance Mary is recorded as having overseen the knitting of thousands of comforts for the troops in the First World War by the women and children of the estate.[29] Sylvia organised similar work in the Second World War, when she and her daughter Pamela worked as Red Cross nurses at nearby Frickley Hospital, together with Minnie Hindle, wife of the estate foreman.[30] Women's energies were also sometimes channelled into political activities. Elizabeth Thellusson was a committee member in 1885, and later 'Dame', of the new Doncaster Habitation of the Primrose League. This organisation was set up to enable women to support the Conservative party after the franchise had been widened and electoral practices tightened.[31]

In addition to these wider duties, the women of the family pursued leisure activities for their own enjoyment and as part of their supportive roles as hostess, companion and wife. Their accomplishments were those of women with no need to support themselves financially, and made them entertaining companions. They included music, needlework and art; several oil paintings in the house are signed by Aline. Social activities often centred round sport, and house-parties were often

FIGURE 7

Constance Mary Thellusson, at the wheel of the SY *Carmela* in about 1905.

ENGLISH HERITAGE

FIGURE 8
This image of the indoor staff at Brodsworth was taken in 1914, after which time staff numbers declined steadily.
EDWARDS FAMILY

held at Brodsworth during the shooting season. Women were spectators for some sports, but took part in others; Brodsworth was equipped with an archery range and croquet lawns. Georgiana loyally lists yachting as her favourite occupation, while Constance Mary, wife of her third son Charles, is to be seen at the wheel of their steam yacht (fig. 7). They often took guests with them on their yacht, and travelled widely. The Grant-Daltons also sailed and skied together, and spent much time at their holiday home on Mull. The house and estate often had to be managed for long periods in the family's absence.

The successful running of the country house depended heavily upon the well-defined and interdependent relationships of family and staff. In addition to her role as hostess, the mistress played a key role in overseeing the running of the household by the domestic staff, who were ultimately responsible to her. The roles of both mistress and housekeeper were likened by Mrs Beeton to that of an army commander. By setting a good example to their staff, with careful planning and co-ordination, they could ensure the moral and physical order of the household.[32] Jane Langton, housekeeper for over twenty years, was both feared and respected by her staff, leaving a legacy of strict discipline. Her successor, Emily Chester, combined the roles of cook and housekeeper for more than fifty years. During this time, the tradition of the daily consultation with the mistress was maintained, but latterly it was Sylvia who went through to the back of the house to meet Emily.

The relationships and hierarchies within the ranks of the staff themselves were equally important in ensuring that the mechanisms of the country house ran smoothly (fig. 8). Under the direction of the housekeeper, cook and butler, were teams of staff whose roles and activities were clearly delineated by rank. The Brodsworth housekeepers' account books illustrate clearly these divisions of status, and the way in which they provided a career structure in which women, who demonstrated the virtues of honesty, sobriety and industry, were able to rise up the ranks of service.[33] Progression was however dependent upon women choosing not

FIGURE 9
Caroline Palmer came to Brodsworth in 1906 as Kitchen Maid. She progressed to become Cook in 1915, and left the following year to marry the Valet Alfred Edwards.
EDWARDS FAMILY

FIGURE 10

Kate Bott was Lady's Maid to
Constance Thellusson from
1906-09. The two women
remained firm friends for the
rest of their lives.

ENGLISH HERITAGE/MURIEL BRAMWELL

to marry (fig. 9). Caroline Palmer came to Brodsworth as kitchen maid in 1906, and rose up the ranks to become cook in 1915, enjoying a corresponding rise from £6 to £10 per quarter which is recorded in the accounts. Her career was curtailed the following year when she married chauffeur Alfred Edwards.[34]

Other staff found their positions within the household less clearly defined. Kate Bott, lady's maid to Constance Mary Thellusson from 1906-09, became a trusted friend and confidante to her mistress, despite the different circumstances of their birth. The two remained in contact for the rest of their lives. In practice, a hierarchical relationship could also become one of friendship (fig. 10).

For the governess, and to some extent the nursery staff, the close contact with the family set them apart from the rest of the domestic staff. Pamela Williams remarked on this uneasy relationship suggesting that, depending on the attitude of the governess, other staff might choose to support or undermine her.[35] Their ambiguous status within the household was reflected in the area of the house in which they spent most time. The nurseries and schoolroom at Brodsworth were situated between the main family rooms and the servants' wing. With its carefully delineated and graduated spaces, the house itself reinforced the hierarchical structures of those who lived and worked within it.

Changes during the twentieth century caused both the hierarchies, and the spatial arrangements which embodied them, to be eroded. The impact of two World Wars contributed to the declining needs and fortunes of country houses. This brought many changes for both women of the family and staff at Brodsworth. The family was forced to reduce expenditure on the building, staff and their way of life. Maintaining the house and her role as its mistress became increasingly difficult for Sylvia, who took a greater personal involvement in its daily management. Her experiences contrasted dramatically with those of her predecessors, the daily struggle to make ends meet now being shared on both sides of the baize door. Staff numbers declined steadily over the course of the century, leaving only Emily resident as cook-housekeeper by 1988. From the 1950s daily cleaning ladies from the village were employed, as well as casual staff for particular occasions. Female staff like Sheila Parkin-Coates, appointed as a parlourmaid, found herself undertaking more general roles, including those of butler and footman, once specifically male.[36] Similar changes in the structure of the outdoor staff were also taking place. Work in the gardens and woods was taken on by women temporarily during the First World War and continued to be undertaken by them afterwards on a more permanent basis.

By the middle of the twentieth century, increasing opportunities for women in other spheres, and poor pay and conditions within service, made it less attractive as a career. The domestic skills it provided, once so highly valued, were no longer deemed necessary in an increasingly technological age. A fundamental shift was also taking place in attitudes as to what was desirable in terms of career, lifestyle and family choices. This is well illustrated by Pamela Williams' choice not to take on the hall, but to move into the former head gardener's house. The benefits of a smaller house with modern technology outweighed the size, grandeur and tradition of the country house.

Old age and widowhood

Widowhood often brought with it change and insecurity for both maids and mistresses. However, advancing years could also bring a degree of independence.

With widowhood came the threat of having to leave their homes for women of the family and the staff alike. The death of the estate owner meant that his widow had to leave the house to make way for his successor. Elizabeth and Constance Mary both enjoyed long lives after leaving Brodsworth, the latter returning to her first married house, Collingwood, in Torquay. Sylvia Grant Dalton was an exception to this, staying on at Brodsworth as 'tenant for life' after her husband's death in 1952. Widows from working families often left their homes, being found more appropriate accommodation by the estate: Minnie Hindle and Lizzie Whitham moved into cottages converted for them in the 1970s.[37]

The families of all these women would play a vital role in providing support. For upper-class women, widowhood was softened by financial provision from the family. Charles Sabine Thellusson paid annuities to several relatives, including £1,000 to his mother for twenty-six years until her death aged eighty-six.[38] For widows from working-class families however, financial assistance came from their employers and landlords. The Thellussons and Grant-Daltons undertook this role seriously and with a considerable degree of compassion, as is demonstrated by the tenant rent lists in the estate accounts. Widows of long-serving estate workers were on several occasions provided with pensions and permitted to stay on in their cottages. Reductions in rent are also recorded in cases where women were unable to pay the sum required.[39]

Other widows were able to able to provide for themselves and their children through taking in work such as ironing or washing or going out to work again on a casual basis.[40] Kate Day found work at the Hall as a kitchen maid for a brief period around 1909-12, and is present in the photograph of the women working in the kitchen taken around that time (fig. 11 and plate 4).

Saving for old age or widowhood for most working families was impossible. For those women however who chose service over marriage, minimal living costs meant they could accumulate significant sums.[41] Years of loyalty were also often rewarded by employers with bequests. Constance Mary left money to two of her maids, Lilian Lipscombe and Clara Jackson, who went down to Collingwood with her in 1919.[42] Pamela Grant-Dalton's last governess Miss Wallace was provided with a cottage in the village in return for years of faithful service.[43]

For many women their experiences in later life were shaped as much by personality as by circumstance. Constance Mary enjoyed a full social life and kept her sense of fun into her old age. Sylvia Grant-Dalton, is also remembered for her indomitable spirit, valiantly continuing her role at the hall in her widowed years.

FIGURE 11
Kate Day came back to work as a Kitchen Maid after being widowed in 1910.

ENGLISH HERITAGE/EDNA TAGG

She stated in her last year, with reference to the formidable Jane Langton: 'I've never been frightened of anyone or anything in my life'.[44]

Conclusions

For most of Brodsworths maids and mistresses, the circumstances of their birth dictated the shape of their lives. While recent research has revealed some previously unidentified parallels, many aspects of their lives were essentially very different. In this, they conformed to the conventions and expectations of their sex and status. The twentieth century brought new opportunities for women, and challenges for country houses. These are reflected at Brodsworth by Sylvia Grant-Dalton's struggle to continue with declining staff numbers. An element of continuity however can also be detected in her strong sense of obligation to the house and to her wider duties, and Emily Chester's unstinting service and loyalty. Brodsworth's women have at last begun to emerge from the shadows. Evidence of their experiences has shed light on them as wives, daughters, mothers and maids, highlighting their vitally important role in the country house community.

1   For further information see Girouard, M., *The Victorian Country House* (New Haven, 1985), pp. 236-42; Wilson, R. and A. Mackley, *Creating Paradise: The Building of the English Country House, 1660-1880* (London, 2000); Carr-Whitworth, C. et al, *Brodsworth Hall and Gardens* (English Heritage, 2000).

2   Doncaster Archives, DDBrod/1–23; Yorkshire Archaeological Society, (YAS) Leeds, DD132 and DD168.

3   Doncaster Archives, DDBrod/11/29, 11/30 and 11/32, 1890-1936.

4   Brodsworth Hall Oral History archive (OH), containing over 30 recordings from 1992 to the present.

5   Polden, P., *Peter Thellusson's Will of 1797 and its Consequences on Chancery Law* (Lewiston, Queenstown, 2002).

6   Polden, *Peter Thellusson's Will*, pp. 385-7; Public Record Office London (PRO), PROB11/2120, Will of William Theobald, 1849; YAS DD168/16, Draft letter from C. S. Thellusson.

7   YAS DD168/2, Philip Wilkinson, architect, London, Building specification, February 1861; DD168/1/11, Estate Accounts, 'Balance of Mr Wilkinson's commission as architect', August 1863.

8   Doncaster Archives DDBrod /3/1, Post-nuptial settlement, and YAS DD168/10, Minutes of G and CSA Thellusson's settlements.

9   Dars, C. (ed.), *Catalogue of Paintings in British Collections* (London, 1993).

10 Purchased from the 1865 Dublin International Exhibition of 1865. YAS DD168/7/1/15-21, Correspondence between Thellusson, Casentini from Lucca who supplied the sculptures, and the Exhibition Company, 1865-6; Read, B., 'Vintage Victoriana', *Country Life*, clxxxiii 8 June 1989, pp. 314-7.

11 Interview with Lucinda Lambton, *Forty Minutes*, BBC, Broadcast 1988.

12 OH, Gladys Jones (née Phillips), 1993.

13 Edwards family archive.

14 YAS DD168/7/1/4, Lapworths Brothers of London, Bill for furnishing Brodsworth, 1863.

15 Doncaster Archives, DDBrod/14/2, the quiz dated 1869.

16 OH, Pamela Williams (née Grant-Dalton), 1994.

17 Doncaster Archives, SR/58/1/1, School Log Book, 1871-1922.

18 Doncaster Archives, SR/58/1/1, School Log Book.

19 Sambrook, P., *The Country House Servant* (Stroud, 1999), p. 244.

20 YAS DD168/1/35. Estate Accounts for 1886.

21 Sheffield Archives 606/F/1.

22 OH, Margaret Handley (née Taylor), 2003; OH, Ernest Spencer, 2003; Tagg correspondence 2003.

23 *St. Dunstans' Review*, 1937.

24 OH, Pamela Williams (née Grant-Dalton), 1994.

25 OH, Margaret Handley (née Taylor), 2003.

26 Gerard, J., 'Lady Bountiful: Women of the Landed Classes and Rural Philanthropy', *Victorian Studies* 30 (1987), pp. 183-207.

27 *Doncaster Chronicle*, 23 November 1900.

28 Doncaster Archives, SR58/1-3, Brodsworth School Log Books 1871-1984; Mary Scott Archive.

29 Undated local newspaper clippings, c. 1916.

30 OH, Molly Nicholls (née Hindle), 2001-2.

31 Rule Book and Certificate, Brodsworth collection; Horn, P., *Ladies of the Manor: Wives and Daughters in Country-house Society, 1830-1918* (Stroud, 1991), pp. 176-8.

32 Mrs Beeton, *Book of Household Management* (London, 1861, 1888 edn.), pp. 1, 6, 20.

33 Mrs Beeton, *Everyday Cookery and Housekeeping Book* (London, 1865,) p. 20.

34 Doncaster Archives, DDBrod/11/29 and 11/30 Housekeepers' Account Books; OH Edwards 1992-2003.

35 OH, Pamela Williams, 1994.

36 OH, Sheila Hopkinson (née Parkin-Coates), 2001-3.

37 OH, Molly Nicholls (née Hindle), 2001-2; OH, Wilf Hindle, 2001-2.

38 YAS, DD168/1/1-33, Estate Accounts, 1865-1884.

39 YAS, DD168/1/34, Estate Accounts for 1885; Mary Newsome, Mary Swift and Mary Smith, all listed by agent Mr Baines as paying reduced rent when unable to pay; OH, Spencer, 2004.

40 Doncaster Archives, DDBrod/11/32, housekeepers' account books record payments to Mrs Sendall for washing and ironing in 1930s. OH, Covell, 2003, Mrs Adams ironing.

41 Probate Registry, York, Jane Langton, (died intestate) 1936.

42 Probate Registry, York, will 1946.

43 OH, Pamela Williams (née Grant-Dalton), 1994.

44 *Forty Minutes*, 1988.

A Soldier's Wife: Lady Chichester

GERARDINE M. MULCAHY

I n the study of the country house, little regard has been paid to the genteel women who married those younger sons of the nobility and gentry who embarked on military careers. The letters and diaries of Lady Chichester offer an account of a rich and varied life as an officer's wife during the first half of the nineteenth century.

Mary Barbara Clifford was born at Tixall Hall, Staffordshire in October 1801 (plate 5 and fig. 1). She was the eldest child of Sir Thomas Hugh Clifford who inherited Burton Constable Hall in East Yorkshire in 1821 and assumed the name Clifford Constable (plate 6). A genteel young woman, 'nursed in all that was Elegant & Splendid',[1] Mary married her cousin Charles Chichester (1795-1847), an army officer and the second son of Charles Joseph Chichester of Calverleigh Court in Devon, in April 1826. It is evident from surviving letters and journals that they had been close since childhood, shared a passion for travelling, and enjoyed a happy and loving marriage.[2] Nevertheless, Charles Chichester was not a prize catch. As was customary for the younger son of a landed gentleman, Charles had embarked on a military career. His allowance from the family's estates in Devon and Ireland was relatively modest,[3] and it seems Mary's settlement was not all they had hoped for. Although the details of the marriage settlement do not survive, a number of letters exchanged between Mary and her future sister-in-law Eliza Chichester refer to the Chichesters' disappointment.[4] Consequently, Charles would be forced to rely on career advancements to provide adequately for a wife and family.

Part way through his education at Stonyhurst, the Roman Catholic seminary near Clitheroe in Lancashire, Charles had pleaded impatience to embark on a military career, and his parents agreed to take him away from school.[5] He was appointed ensign in the 14th Regiment of Foot in March 1811 and initially stationed in Malta (plate 8). In December that year, he received a letter from his uncle, Sir Thomas Hugh Clifford, in which he is warned of the pitfalls of military life:

… your Mother complains much of your extravagance, I am sadly afraid you should get an itching for gambling which would bring you to ruin very shortly. George Fitzherbert informed me that most of the Officers did nothing but gamble all day long & that sometimes they took hold of him & endeavoured to push him to the table by force, but he always found means to escape … he gave me so much satisfaction that I took great pains to have him made a Lieutenant, and I hope you will give me reason to be as satisfied with you.[6]

Without doubt, money and influence were the most effective means of securing advancement in military service.[7] It is likely that Charles received a portion of his entitlement from the family before he came of age. This, coupled with the influence of his wealthy uncle (and future father-in-law) Thomas Hugh Clifford, undoubtedly secured 'advancement', and Charles was made a lieutenant of the 14th Regiment of Foot the following year.[8]

Mary did not travel with Charles in their first years of marriage. Having been promoted to major, Charles was active with the 60th regiment, for a time serving in North America,[9] and as their early years of marriage were marred by infant mortality, it was wiser for Mary to remain at Calverleigh, the Chichester family home in Devon. Their first child, Mary Isabella, was born in Portsmouth, possibly as Mary accompanied Charles to his port of embarkation as he set out on his next tour of duty.[10] The child died three months later, but within a few short months Mary was pregnant again. The sense of loss following the death of their second child[11] was compounded when, shortly after, Mary's younger sister Isabella died – probably in childbirth.[12] It was therefore with understandable relief that Charles wrote to 'aunt Constantia' from Portsmouth following the birth of their third child in January 1830:

> *My Dear Constantia*
>
> *you will be delighted to hear that D[ea]r Mary's troubles are over, she was brought to bed last night of a son they are both doing well as possible he is to be called Charles Raleigh … this is the eleventh letter I have written today … I am too tired to write more.*[13]

Although Charles had regular leave, Mary found the long periods of enforced separation trying. Charles was a keen correspondent, but in May 1831, prompted by loneliness, Mary wrote: 'If you knew my dearest Charles the delight I experience in receiving your letters you would not begrudge the trouble it gives you to write them'.[14] Mary had been ill, evidently following the birth of another child. Her past experiences had made her fearful, as she explained:

> *Mr Middleton came to see me yesterday and says I must begin to walk by degrees in 3 or 4 days time & go out on the balcony & walk about the room. I am very well but I intend to be over careful tho I am longing to walk to see my Baby & I do not know which will carry this day, my fears or my impetuosity.*[15]

The child, Thomas Arthur Pigott, died the following July at Calverleigh.[16]

In July 1831, Charles obtained a lieutenant-colonelcy, unattached.[17] There followed a relative lull in his military career, and for a time he was tempted to dabble in politics. They remained at Calverleigh, where Mary gave birth to their son Hugh Arthur in February 1833, and a daughter Mary Honoria, the following year.[18] However, 'tired to death of ... idle life,' in June 1835 Charles prepared to joined the British auxiliary legion fighting in Spain in the First Carlist War.[19]

Whilst in London in June 1835, Charles heard a rumour that they were enlisting 'men and officers for the service of the Queen of Spain'.[20] Consequently, he spoke to Lord Palmerston who confirmed the rumour and, furthermore, gave him a letter of introduction to the Spanish ambassador, who was responsible for overseeing the appointment of officers.[21] Charles applied for the post of brigadier-general. If he proved successful he would not only further his hopes of promotion in the British Army on his eventual return from Spain, but also secure his financial position in the interim. The auxiliary legion had the consent of the British government, so alongside his full pay as a brigadier-general in the service of Spain, Charles would continue to receive half pay as lieutenant-colonel in the British service.[22]

Despite having three young children, there was no question of Mary remaining at home. Nevertheless, Charles had concerns for her safety, and although travelling to Spain may not be 'advisable... the South of France, Toulouse, or Bayonne, might perhaps do'.[23] But, for the moment there were more pressing matters. If Charles gained the appointment as brigadier-general, they must make appropriate financial arrangements. He wrote:

> ... you must write to Clifford for our money most urgently, we may want it ... [there] would of course be a good deal of expense in fitting out, I should probably want another horse, perhaps 2; and if am detained in Town, I should wish you to come up. then again there will be uniforms &c.&c.[24]

As a military wife, Mary had learnt to be prudent with money, and at this crucial time, 'dearest Mary' would appreciate how 'fortunate' it was that she had been so.[25] The following day, Charles got news that he had successfully gained the appointment and was anxious to tell Mary all:

> *My Dearest Mary*
>
> *I am a Brigadier General in the service of Spain. I got a notification to that effect today ... the pay is to be British (I don't know what a Brigadier is in our Service) and I am told, though I don't believe it is quite positive, we receive if we retire after 6 months service, a gratuity of a years pay, of two years after twelve months service, & so on. We retain our rank in the British Service.[26]*

With these assurances in mind, Mary made the necessary financial arrangements and began the search for suitable serving staff to accompany them. Charles was especially anxious that she secure a young groom as his present groom, Norman, was rather long-in-the-tooth and would 'never stand the knocking about which in all probability we shall have'. He would appreciate it if Mary could break the news to Norman, and search out 'a stout young fellow' in his place.[27]

There were arrangements to be made regarding uniform and Charles asked

FIGURE 2

San Sebastian from the convent of St. Francesco May 1836, attributed to Lady Chichester, 1836, watercolour.

BURTON CONSTABLE HALL

Mary to gather together his pistols, his 'red uniform epaulettes', his dress uniform 'with swords sashes &c.', and his saddles and bridles and 'get all ... packed'. Since Charles had little faith in Spanish horses, he asked Mary to look out for a new horse which 'must have blood or it will not stand the fatigue'.[28]

Mary remained at Calverleigh for some weeks, busy with the necessary arrangements. Charles had implored, that if she could bear the journey to London, he was desperate to see her and the children before he set out for San Sebastian in Spain.[29] However, he felt it advisable the baby, Mary Honoria, should remain at Calverleigh,[30] and so Mary set out for London with the two boys, Charles Raleigh, then five years old and Arthur, barely two-and-a-half. As Charles was to be amongst the first detachments of the British auxiliary legion to set sail for San Sebastian, within days, Mary, Charles and the two children left London for Plymouth (fig. 2).[31]

Passage aboard troopships was notoriously gruesome.[32] Thankfully, as an officer's wife, Mary would not have to succumb to the rigours of regimental transport, as she could afford to pay for her own, more comfortable passage.[33] It was evidently too dangerous for Mary and the children to join Charles in Spain, and it was decided she should travel to the south of France. As Bayonne was only three hours away by steamer from San Sebastian, it seemed the favoured place,[34] although, once Charles was settled, Mary and the children were to join him in Spain.[35]

It appears Mary initially travelled to Dieppe, before setting out for Pau, north of the Pyrenees.[36] It was undoubtedly a painful decision to leave Mary Honoria at home, but having already suffered three infant deaths, she must have felt her baby daughter would be safer in England.

There are few details of Mary's accommodation in the Pyrenees, although it was probably quite comfortable.[37] Charles joined them at Pau when he could,[38] and at other times Mary travelled to Paris, where she stayed at the Hotel de Londres, possibly in the company of her family.[39] It appears she sat for her portrait to Claude-Marie Dubufe (1790-1864) during one of these excursions (plate 7).[40]

In April 1837, their baby daughter Mary Honoria died. Mary may have travelled back to Yorkshire for a time as the child was buried at Burton Constable.[41] However, she was certainly back in France the following month.[42] Heavily pregnant, she remained in Paris, where she gave birth to a son, Henry Sebastian, on 5 July that year.[43] Although Charles wrote regularly from the front line, his letters, with their graphic accounts of battle, could offer little comfort and must have left Mary in fear for his life. The loss of their daughter, her concern for their young sons and the perils of childbirth made for exceptionally trying years.

With the original auxiliary legion disbanded, Charles returned home in late 1837. As a distinguished and gallant hero, he had been commended for his services to the Queen of Spain with the Grand Cross of San Fernando, and the third and first class decorations of Isabella the Catholic and Charles III.[44] By the close of 1837, Charles had volunteered for the colonial army sent to quell the uprisings in Upper and Lower Canada, and Mary and the children joined him in 'the wilds of British North America'.[45] They remained in Canada for two years and their daughter, Mary Constantia, was born at Toronto on 6 October 1839.[46] Later that month Charles was appointed lieutenant-colonel of the 81st Regiment of Foot, and began the year 1840 'under orders for England, to take command of the 81st now on their way ... [to] Barbados'.[47]

The couple faced a long and arduous journey from Canada with their three sons and baby daughter. Henry Sebastian was taken ill and Mary suspected he had an 'inflammation of the lungs', although Charles was more optimistic and inclined to believe the child had little more than a cold. Unfortunately, Sebastian's condition deteriorated rapidly and with inadequate medical provision on board ship, they were forced to wait until they docked at Cork, in Ireland, before Charles could rush ashore for a doctor. Mary's fears were confirmed, and the doctor pronounced 'an almost hopeless case of inflammation of the lungs!'.[48] The child died and was buried at Cork. Charles wrote in his journal:

Gods Holy Will be done. but it is a severe blow. just the age to have acquired all one's fondness. how proud I was of him: how pretty he looked the last time he came playing upon deck & how little I thought I was so soon to lose him. could we have had medical advice it might perhaps have been stopped. but now there is every reason to fear it is too late. it has lasted at least 5 days: caught I fear by his having been allowed to lie sleeping one day on the cabin floor when the skylight was off: Mary said at once it was inflammation of the lungs; I could not believe it, would to God I had. and though we could do but little, that little a day sooner might have saved him.[49]

When they arrived in England, Mary set out for Burton Constable and Charles remained in London in order to approach his commanding officer and request an extended leave of absence.[50] The family

FIGURE 3
Burton Constable Hall, West Front, Sir Thomas Aston Clifford Constable, c. 1850, pencil sketch, Lady Chichester's Scrapbook.
BURTON CONSTABLE HALL

had endured trying years, and grief stricken at the loss of her 'dear little Sebastian',[51] Mary needed a break from the relentless tours of duty. Despite initial objections,[52] Charles secured an extended period of leave, and joined Mary and the children at Burton Constable (fig. 3).[53] However, he had one rather important event to attend before he set out.

Having been honoured by Queen Isabella for his heroic service in Spain, Charles was knighted by Queen Victoria, at St. James's Palace. On 6 April 1840, he wrote to Mary:

My Lady

It is all over, I never was in such a fright in my life … there was no sword ready, and there I was upon my knee, waiting till Lord Hill brought his. Who was present, God in Heaven knows. I wanted to see Prince Albert and he might have been at Burton Constable. Philip Howard & his father were before me, but when they found out what it was, they made me go first to have a laugh. I am off tomorrow and shall get to you as quick as I can.[54]

Despite feeling 'low and melancholy', Mary and the family determined to make the most of their time in England.[55] Accompanied by their usual 'heap of luggage',[56] they relaxed into country house living at Burton Constable and enjoyed the usual round of entertainment: hunting, shooting, and even the spectacle on offer at the York Assizes where Mary's brother, Sir Thomas Aston Clifford Constable, oversaw a number of cases as High Sheriff including '6 murders & as many rapes'.[57]

By the autumn, the family were ready to leave England for Barbados, where Charles was to join his regiment. Once again Mary was pregnant, and together with her young family, faced the long and arduous voyage to the West Indies. However, having endured the harsh Canadian winters, Mary delighted in the West Indies from the outset. A year after their arrival, she recorded in her diary that, despite her 'delicate condition' on arrival, she was thankful that they had all enjoyed such good health, especially Amy, her little 'Trinidadian', born in March 1841, who was the very 'picture of health'.[58]

A foreign posting did not necessarily mean going to war, and the family might look forward to pleasurable years abroad. Their time in the West Indies was most agreeable for the Chichesters, moving freely between Barbados and Trinidad. Charles's regiment was stationed at St. James's barracks in Trinidad, and although officers sometimes chose to live in barracks, it was not a requirement.[59] As a married officer, Charles and his family took a house a mile or so away from camp and he would walk to the barracks daily. There was good medical provision available for the army wives and their children, and not only was their baby daughter born at St. James's barracks[60], but Mary also records collecting medicine from the barracks as needed when the children were ill.[61]

Mary was deeply committed to her Catholic faith and in Trinidad she could attend Mass regularly and with relative ease.[62] As was customary, she had a retinue of servants, including a nanny. A number of the servants accompanied Mary from England, although some must have been recruited locally. It appears she felt frustrated with the 'black servants' in Trinidad, and at times considered them 'intolerable'.[63]

The etiquette of 'calling' on appropriate neighbours and friends was not dissimilar to the customs of polite society in England.[64] Polite entertainment was readily available, including fancy dress balls,[65] dinner parties (with 'charades')[66] and the ubiquitous regimental band.[67] Nevertheless, there were significant differences, including the opportunity to go country house visiting Venezuelan style.

Having crossed from the Port of Spain, on 21 December 1841, Sir Charles and Lady Chichester were amongst the guests invited to Señor Escucheria's country house – Il Paraiso.[68] On approaching the house they were greeted by the Señor and a number of ladies, elegantly dressed with 'rings, diamonds & pearls on every finger even on thumbs.' General Paëz, President of Venezuela, was guest of honour (fig. 4). However, having found herself in awe of the ladies' appearance, Mary was less impressed with their manners. She wrote:

> … they treat him [General Paëz] with but little ceremony, the Ladies receive him like any other man – sitting – the gentlemen even sit whilst he stands talking to them … I like respect to be shown 'to the powers that be'.

Nevertheless, Mary found herself surprisingly impressed by their musical talent and delighted in the 'very splendid' food, which included '2 magnificent fish' and 'profusion of good things' for dessert.

There was much to see and do on their excursion to Venezuela including a visit to a coffee estate, and an encounter with horsemen in pursuit of a bull, which should have been performing at a bull fight in the nearby town of Patau.[69] Yet, Mary was anxious to get back to the children,[70] and so they prepared to leave Caracas on horseback as far as La Guaria, from where they would take the boat to Trinidad. Although she was an accomplished horsewoman, the terrain was harsh and the journey made more difficult by riding side-saddle along narrow, precipitous paths, over roads she describes as barely 'traced'. They eventually reached the Neptuno Hotel, where they broke their journey, 'breakfasted, [and] paid a visit to Miss Renshaw the daughter of the American Consul' before returning to Trinidad.[71]

Their next few weeks at Trinidad were marred by uncertainty, as they patiently endured the discomfort and inconvenience of 'having half … [their] furniture packed up' whilst awaiting notification of the impending move to Antigua.[72] Their uncertainty was no doubt exacerbated by rumours that Charles was to be appointed acting governor of Trinidad.[73] After a short spell in Antigua, they returned to Trinidad, where, in August that year, Charles was indeed appointed acting governor.[74]

On 10 May 1843, Mary gave birth to her tenth child. The boy was born prematurely at Bridgetown, Barbados, and died the same day. Mary had evidently

FIGURE 4

'Flowers from General Paëz, President of Venezuela's garden, Caracas Decr 1841. given me by himself', Lady Chichester's Scrapbook.

BURTON CONSTABLE HALL

been unwell for a day or two, and had asked Charles to cancel their impending social engagements. She records:

Wednesday – I had great difficulty to get a room arranged for me in time – a little Boy was born about half past ten in the morning he lived about half an hour & I had the Happiness of having him Baptized [sic] by Casey – He was buried in the Catholic's burying ground that even[ing] by Mr Rogers.[75]

FIGURE 5
St. John's Barracks Canada East,
H. E. Sorell, 81st Regt., 1846,
watercolour.
BURTON CONSTABLE HALL

She makes no further reference to this sad event in her diary, and it appears that within a day or two life continued as before. Despite eventually giving birth to eleven children (only five of which survived to adulthood), Mary was reluctant to record details of her pregnancies, births or even her pain and sense of loss at the death of a child. Nevertheless, we should not underestimate her difficulties and discomfort as she journeyed from place to place, often heavily pregnant. Nor should we underestimate her grief, although, as a devote Catholic, her faith in God doubtless offered comfort.[76]

In August 1843 the Chichesters arrived in Quebec,[77] where Charles took up his post at St. John's barracks, Montreal (fig. 5). Following extended leave at Burton Constable in 1845, they moved to Toronto, where Mary gave birth to her youngest son Henry Augustus Talbot during the oppressively hot summer of 1846.[78] While awaiting news of their next posting,[79] Charles was taken ill and died on 4 April 1847. He had complained of 'violent pains' a few days earlier, and was seen by the doctor, but deteriorated rapidly (fig. 6).

FIGURE 6
Sir Charles Chichester in death, attributed to Lady Chichester, 1847, pastel.
BURTON CONSTABLE HALL

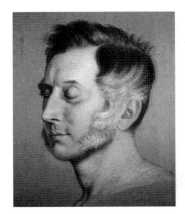

Following the death of her husband, Mary and the children returned home to England and Burton Constable. It was decided that she should live in the dower house, Wood Hall.[80] Despite her trials as a soldier's wife, Mary's life had never been dull. With her passion for travel far from abated, Mary could not settle to sedentary life. She was in Paris for the early days of the 1848 Revolution, where she 'fell in with a band of armed populace' returning from Sacre Couer.[81] She travelled extensively throughout Europe in the following years and made her final trip to the continent at the age of seventy-one.[82] She died on 14 December 1876 in her London home at Ovington Gardens, South Kensington.[83]

1   Hull University Library (HUL), Chichester papers, DDCH/36, Letter from Lady Bedingfeld to Mary Barbara Chichester (later Lady Chichester), c. 1826.

2   See HUL, DDCH/86, Diary of Mary Barbara Clifford Constable (later Lady Chichester) 1822-1824. Also, Mulcahy, G., '"A Fine Soldier" – Sir Charles Chichester (1795-1847)', in the forthcoming edition of *Leeds Museums and Galleries Review*, 2004.

3   HUL, DDCH/36, Letter from Honoria Chichester to her son Charles Chichester (later Sir Charles Chichester), 28 May 1831.

4   East Riding Archive Office (ERAO), Chichester Constable papers, DDCC 144/31, Letters from Mary Barbara Clifford Constable to Miss Eliza Chichester, 12 March 1826 and 23 March 1826.

5   HUL, DDCH/36, Letter from Sir Thomas Hugh Clifford (later Clifford Constable) to Charles Chichester, 1 December 1811.

6   ibid.

7   See Thompson, F. M. L., *English Society in the Nineteenth Century* (London, 1963), p. 72.

8   ibid.

9   Manners Chichester, H., 'Chichester, Sir Charles (1795-1847)', in Lislie, S. (ed.), *Dictionary of National Biography* (London, 1887), p. 256. Sir Thomas Hugh Clifford Constable died in 1823 but was undoubtedly aware of the proposed marriage between his daughter Mary and his nephew Charles Chichester.

10   HUL, DDCH/22, 'Summary of the Career of Sir Charles Chichester' by Lady Chichester, 1847.

11   ibid.

12   Mary Isabella married Henry Raymond Arundel on 27 September 1827. She died with issue eleven months later.

13   HUL, DDCH/38, Letter from Charles Chichester to Constantia Clifford, 12 February 1830. The letter is dated 12 February 1830 – an error, no doubt caused by the writer's fatigue! Charles Raleigh was born on the 11 January 1830 (see HUL, DDCH/22).

14   HUL, DDCH/36, Letter from Mary Barbara Chichester to Charles Chichester, 4 May 1831.

15   ibid.

16   HUL, DDCH/22, 'Summary of the Career of Sir Charles Chichester' by Lady Chichester, 1847.

17   Manners Chichester, H., *Dictionary of National Biography*, p. 256.

18   HUL, DDCH/22.

19   HUL, DDCH/75, Diary of Sir Charles Chichester 1835-7, 17 July 1835. When Ferdinand VII of Spain died in September 1833, his wife Maria Christina became Queen Regent on behalf of their three-year-old daughter Isabella. Convinced that he was rightful heir to the throne, Ferdinand's brother – don Carlos – disputed Isabella's right to succeed. As a consequence Spain was divided. Two factions arose – the Cristinos (or Isabelinos) and the Carlists. The Cristinos were the supporters of the Queen Regent and her government. The Carlists were the supporters of don Carlos. With the suspension of the Foreign Enlistment Bill, the British Government offered support, albeit half-heartedly, to the Queen of Spain. I am most grateful to Michael Boyd for sharing his research and views on the First Carlist War.

20   HUL, DDCH/75, 17 July 1835.

21   ibid.

22   Burton Constable Hall, Chichester Letters, Letter from Charles Chichester to Mary Barbara Chichester, 10 June 1835. I am most grateful to Mrs Lorna Haysom for transcribing a series of letters from the archive at Burton Constable.

23   ibid.

24   ibid. 'Clifford' is Mary's brother, Sir Thomas Aston Clifford Constable (1806-70) of Burton Constable Hall.

25   ibid.

26   Burton Constable Hall, Letter from Charles Chichester to Mary Barbara Chichester, 11 June 1835.

27   ibid.

28   ibid.

29   ibid.

30   ibid, 14 June 1835.

31   HUL, DDCH/75, 17 July 1835.

32   See Bamfield, V., *On the Strength: The Story of the British Army Wife* (London & Tonbridge, 1974), pp. 29ff. Conditions did improve in the latter half of the nineteenth century. However, as Bamfield explains 'there was still a big difference between the accommodation of the ladies and the wives.' Ibid, p. 36.

33   For the horrors of regimental transport, see Holmes, R., *Redcoat: The British Soldier in the Age of Horse and Musket* (London, 2002).

34 Burton Constable Hall, Letter from Charles Chichester to Mary Barbara Chichester, 18 July 1835.

35 ibid, 30 July 1835.

36 ibid, Letter from Charles Chichester to Mary Barbara at 'Dieppe', 18 July 1835.

37 It was usual for officers to make their own arrangements and their accommodation was usually comfortable, see Bamfield, *On the Strength*, p. 22.

38 Burton Constable Hall, Letter from General De Lacy Evans to Charles Chichester at Pau, July 1837.

39 HUL, DDCH/41, Letter from Charles Chichester to Mary Barbara Chichester, 18 May 1836.

40 The portrait was one of a series of family portraits commissioned for the Clifford Constable's London home at Cumberland Place in c1836-7. Charles Chichester visited Cumberland Place in 1840. He records '... to Cumberland place to see Mary's picture. I cannot say how disappointed I was, it has neither her face, figure, or attitude – as complete a failure as possible. It is not in my opinion even a pretty picture, it gives the idea of a prim, foolish, women who was looking good with all her might & main. Raleigh & Arthur I cannot speak of so positively, children change so much it is not like them now, but may have been very much so when it was done... I left the house in a regular sulky mood... and stalked off to my dinner at the club' (DDCH/78, Diary of Sir Charles Chichester 1840-41, 13 March 1840).

41 HUL, DDCH/22, 'Summary of the Career of Sir Charles Chichester' by Lady Chichester, 1847.

42 HUL, DDCH/41, Letter from Charles Chichester to Mary Barbara Chichester in Paris, 14 May 1837.

43 HUL, DDCH/22.

44 Manners Chichester, H., *Dictionary of National Biography*, p. 256.

45 I am most grateful to Helen Roberts, the archivist at Hull University Library, for access to her unpublished entry on Lady Chichester for the forthcoming *Dictionary of National Biography*.

46 HUL, DDCH/77, Diary of Charles Chichester October 1838-January 1840, 6 October 1839.

47 HUL, DDCH/78, Diary of Sir Charles Chichester 1840-41, 8 January 1840.

48 ibid.

49 ibid.

50 ibid, 13 March 1840.

51 Mary refers to her 'great grief' in her diary entry for the 25 February 1842, the first anniversary of Sebastian's death (DDCH/87 Diary of Lady Chichester 1841-1844).

52 Burton Constable Hall, Letter from Charles Chichester to Mary Barbara Chichester, 17 March 1840.

53 HUL, DDCH/78, 8 April 1840.

54 Burton Constable Hall, Letter to Mary Barbara from Sir Charles Chichester dated 6 April 1840.

55 ibid, 17 March 1840.

56 HUL, DDCH/78, 10 July 1840.

57 ibid.

58 HUL, DDCH/87, 8 March 1842.

59 See Bamfield, V., *On the Strength*, p. 23.

60 HUL, DDCH/22.

61 See HUL, DDCH/87, 22 March 1842.

62 Mary records attending mass on numerous occasions, see for example HUL, DDCH/87, 9, 23, 30 January 1842, 6 February 1842.

63 ibid, 22 January 1842.

64 See Bamfield, *On the Strength*, p. 204

65 HUL, DDCH/87, 7 February 1842.

66 HUL, DDCH/80, Diary of Sir Charles Chichester October 1842 - December 1843, 10 May 1843.

67 HUL, DDCH/87, 13 March 1842.

68 HUL, DDCH/87, 21 December 1841.

69 ibid, 28 December 1841

70 ibid, 22, 30 December 1841.

71 ibid, 31 December 1841.

72 ibid, 3 February 1842.

73 ibid, 20 March 1842.

74 For their time in Antigua see HUL, DDCH/87, February 1842.

75 ibid, 10 May 1843.

76 It would appear Mary was far from unique in her hesitation to offer detailed accounts of pregnancy and childbirth. Katie Hickman notes that 'Diplomatic women of the eighteenth and early nineteenth centuries are generally far more open on the delicate subject of childbirth than their successors. Mary Scheil, writing in the mid-nineteenth century, does not allude directly either to her pregnancies or to the births of her children.' Hickman, K., *Daughters of Britannia: The Lives and Times of Diplomatic Wives,* (London, 2000), p. 236.

77 Roberts, Helen, unpublished entry on Lady Chichester for the forthcoming *Dictionary of National Biography*.

78 See Burton Constable Hall, Letter from Charles Chichester to his son Arthur, 8 July 1846.

79 Charles suspected they would be posted to Ireland (Burton Constable Hall, Letter from Sir Charles Chichester to his son Arthur Chichester, 15 March 1847).

80 HUL, DDCH/89/2, Diary of Lady Chichester 1848, 3 November 1848.

81 ibid, 25 February 1848.

82 Roberts, unpublished entry on Lady Chichester.

83 ibid.

Isabella, fourth Countess of Carlisle:
No Life by Halves

CHRISTOPHER RIDGWAY

The story of Isabella, fourth Countess of Carlisle has been represented as that of a fickle woman and a fruitless life. Widowed in 1758, her second marriage to a man much younger than herself quickly foundered, she then took herself off to live in France, caused embarrassment to her family, experienced financial difficulties, and became enamoured with a French confidence man. She fits perfectly the stereotype of the fortunate woman who threw everything away.[1] Her private life may suggest an emotional turbulence but her documentary life challenges this view. Her correspondence, household accounts, recipe book, and her published volume, *Thoughts in the Form of Maxims Addressed to Young Ladies on Their First Establishment in the World* (1789), offer a wholly different perspective. A closer investigation of this material reveals a more interesting and accomplished figure.[2]

Born in 1721, Isabella was the daughter of William, fourth Lord Byron of Newstead Abbey, Nottinghamshire (plate 9). In time she was to be great aunt to the famous Romantic poet George Gordon, sixth Lord Byron who was born in 1788, seven years before her death.[3] In 1743, aged twenty-two, she married a man more than twice her age, Henry Howard, fourth Earl of Carlisle, who had been widowed a year earlier. Carlisle's loneliness and desperation was compounded by the fact that between 1741 and 1743 he lost all three sons by his first marriage. Of his two daughters the eldest, Arabella, died within three years; only one child, Diana, lived to old age. The pressing need for an heir prompted the Earl to remarry so swiftly, but it is likely that he was captivated by this young woman (plate 10). In her portrait of the late-1730s, painted by the artist Michael Dahl towards the end of his career, the adolescent Isabella has a somewhat ungainly appearance with rustic cheeks and a prominent jaw. She cannot be classed a great beauty, but there is something animated about her presence: a willowy figure, with engaging large brown eyes, strands of hair trail behind her head as if caught in a breeze; her gown also appears to be billowing, and in both hands she holds sprays of white flowers, which offset her long tapering fingers. The portrait offers a clue as to her character,

So, we'll go no more a roving

Lord Byron

35

there is the suggestion of an independent and lively mind in this young woman. In 1743 Lady Mary Wortley Montagu identified this element of individuality when she wrote censoriously, 'I know the young Lady Carlisle. She is very agreeable, but if I am not mistaken in her Inclinations, they are very gay'.[4]

In dynastic terms the marriage with Carlisle was a success. It lasted fifteen years until his death in 1758, during which time Isabella gave birth to four daughters and one son, Frederick the future fifth Earl; all lived to old age (plate 11). Whilst chatelaine at Castle Howard Isabella supervised domestic expenditure, and a volume of accounts for 1744-55 reveals just how detailed was her grasp of affairs. The volume is an abstract of the household accounts (the steward's accounts recording daily transactions in more detail do not survive), and it remains the principal record of domestic expenditure for this period, documenting 'expence during our being away and also our stay at Castle Howard'.[5] The comprehensive nature of the abstract indicates that Isabella was concerned with overall patterns of expenditure and household consumption, and not just for when the family was in residence in Yorkshire.

The summaries divide into weekly periods and list the principal items purchased – wines, groceries, meat, bread and drink, fire and candles, kitchen provisions – and their totals (fig. 1). Alongside these entries are various marginal comments. In June 1744 she jotted down, 'Note Claret now rat'd at 4s 6d per bottle'; a fortnight later she recorded a specific seasonal cost, '7 hogsheads of small beer us'd during ye Harvest'; in the summer of 1745 extra quantities of beef were for when 'we had company'; in 1746 she registered the prices for veal, rabbits, sweetbreads and lean chickens; a year later she remarked that lemons were 'half a crown a dozen'; and in 1754 she recorded the price of salmon and eels, at 6d and 4d per pound respectively (fig. 2).[6]

Each autumn the family would quit Yorkshire, a small core of trusted servants would take care of the house during their absence, and costs would be scaled down. This annual family hiatus would be recorded, as would Isabella's resumption of the accounts on her return, invariably marked by the same summary; thus for 1749, 'The Family left Castle Howard Tuesday ye 7th of November 1749, and return'd thither April ye 24th 1750, in this absence the expence in all articles amounted to £43-6-7'.[7] Variations would also be recorded, for example when the children returned to Castle Howard a month prior to their parents in May 1749; more detailed breakdowns were sometimes provided as when the total of £87-13s-6d, for the period from November 1751 to May 1752 was broken down into 'the expence of coals, soap, candles and charcoal'.[8] Errors would be picked up and corrected; and sub-totals entered, thus during their seven months residency from May to November 1744, the total household expenditure was £912-11s-9d. This compared with a total of £39-14s-4d for the five months the family were away between November 1744 and May 1745 – a reduction in household expenses of something in the order of 95 per cent.[9]

At first sight it is not easy to associate the awkward-looking adolescent in the

Dahl portrait with this meticulous domestic supervisor, but these accounts reveal a confident grasp of arithmetic as well as a trained and ordered mind: a consistent format is followed throughout the volume, the handwriting is neat and legible, there are very few cancellations or errors. Not only had she been taught these principles of housekeeping, but she had absorbed this knowledge and was able to put it to efficient use. Because this volume is an abstract of expenditure this does not mean that Isabella was unconcerned with the minutiae of daily expenditure; her marginal notes testify to the contrary. Today we would describe these summaries as management accounts, and her review of expenditure is at that senior level; the figures enable her to compare quantities and prices, as well as weekly, monthly and annual variations. This volume tells us more about Isabella than her portrait by Dahl; evidently she was someone who took care and pride in her supervision of the household. Thus it comes as no surprise to find among her *Maxims* the following recommendation: 'Observe the utmost regularity in the keeping of your household accounts; it is tranquillity to you; justice to your dependents'.[10]

FIGURE 2

A marginal note on expenditure, detailing the prices of veal, butter, rabbits, sweet breads and lean chickens, made by Isabella in her Abstract of the House Accounts in 1746.

CASTLE HOWARD ARCHIVES

Such tranquillity was to be short-lived for Isabella. In 1758 she was widowed. She was well provided for by the terms of her husband's will, too generously in the opinion of Lady Mary Montagu, who remarked:

> *I am sorry for Lord Carlisle. He was my Friend as well as acquaintance, and a Man of uncommon Probity and good nature. I think he shew'd it by the disposition of his Will in favour of a Lady he had no reason to esteem. It is certainly the kindest thing he could do for her, to endeavour to save her from her own Folly, which would probably have precipitately hurry'd her into a second marriage, which would most surely have reveng'd all her misdemeanours.[11]*

It is not clear what these misdemeanours were, but they must have been the consequence of those gay inclinations that Montagu had identified some years earlier. Masculine opinion of Isabella was rather different, and Henry Seymour Conway declared Isabella to be 'the youngest, handsomest and wittiest widow in England', recommending her as a bride to his friend Horace Walpole.[12]

Within a year Isabella chose to re-marry, and risked forfeiting her jointure, custody of her children, and the executorship of her husband's estate while her eldest son was still a minor. Her second husband, the barrister and antiquary Sir William Musgrave (1735-1800), was fourteen years her younger, prompting Walpole to observe that 'in consideration of the match and of her having years to spare, she has made him a present of ten, and calls him three and thirty'.[13] Isabella's female contemporaries took a less charitable view of the union; Lady Blandford reportedly condemning her for marrying 'a young fellow she must buy breeches for'.[14] This set the tone for much of the subsequent commentary, her behaviour was viewed with a mixture of pity and contempt; this perception has also informed, erroneously, the modern understanding of Isabella.

Shortly after her marriage to Musgrave, Isabella sat for a second portrait by Thomas Gainsborough (Plate 12).[15] Her fine blue gown with lace trimmings denotes wealth and status; the grey hair visible below her cap, may be real or it may be powdered; her expression is commanding. The portrait depicts a mature woman (she was aged thirty-nine); she appears assured, confident in her abilities as mistress of an aristocratic household. But this likeness was made at just the moment when she had chosen to forfeit her independence as a widow; by marrying again she had subordinated herself legally, and to some extent economically, to her new husband. Beneath the calm surface of this image lay a less ordered personal life.

If Isabella was expecting a vivacious life with the younger Musgrave she was mistaken, as he was a sober character given to scholarly pursuits. The marriage was not a success, and many years later the fifth Earl recalled how quarrels and disputes blighted family life at Castle Howard: 'my maternal home was comfortless from domestic feuds; my mother having married a person to whose manners and habits she could not accommodate herself'.[16]

At what point Isabella left Castle Howard for good is unknown. The marriage carried on in name rather than anything else; the couple were reported as sharing a house in London in 1768, but it was not until a year later that they formally separated.[17] Her movements in the 1760s are not always clear, and the evidence is contradictory. Possibly she was in Paris in 1765; between 1767 and 1768 she was in London, agitating to secure marriages for her two daughters Frances and Anne; and she may have been in Florence in 1768.[18] What is certain is that by the end of the 1760s, having formally separated from Musgrave, Isabella chose to be mistress of herself. She decided to leave England, embarking on a peripatetic existence in France, Italy and Switzerland that would last thirteen years.

In the eyes of her contemporaries she was described as a restless, vain and foolish woman. Thus for example, in September 1770, her younger contemporary, sometime friend-cum-rival, and fellow widow, Lady Mary Coke (1727–1811), on receiving the news of Isabella's impending departure from London, surmised in her journal, 'She told me her health and her friend Mrs Howard are her motives for going to Aix, some people think she has another'. Two months later Coke referred to her as 'a certain Countess … not famous for her constancy'. Prurient speculation soon yielded real intelligence, and in September 1771 Coke recorded:

The report you mention of the Dowager is a frightful one, yet I fear not unlikely to be true: I never thought travelling a safe thing for her, especially in the South of France, tho' one shou'd have thought at her age, & with no great pretention to beauty, few temptations wou'd have offer'd to have disgraced herself, for it was always to be fear'd if they did present, they wou'd not be resisted.[19]

The nature of Coke's disapprobation was twofold, Isabella had formed an unsuitable attachment, but she was also encouraging her youngest daughter in an equally inappropriate alliance. Coke was astonished to learn of plans for 'an extraordinary marriage that Ly Julie [sic] Howard is likely to make with an Officer Abroad: a more prudent person then Ly Carlisle might have been of use on this occasion, but unhappily She is so indulgent to the passion of Love, that it makes her a bad adviser on these occasions'.[20]

The root of all these problems lay in that apparent character flaw that had been commented on by Lady Mary Montagu years earlier. Isabella was gay, precipitant, guilty of folly and misdemeanours, inconstant, imprudent, indulgent, her behaviour was disgraceful: all these epithets were marshalled dismissively by Isabella's female contemporaries.[21] This criticism testifies to the difficulty her peers had in accepting her irregular behaviour. Although Isabella journeyed south in search of a warm climate and inexpensive living, there is no doubt that France offered a more congenial moral climate too, as she remarked in 1771, 'I must be absolutely out of the world in England to be well'.[22]

But there is another image of Isabella to be considered. Between October 1771 and January 1773, whilst residing in Provence and the Languedoc she wrote a series of letters to her youngest daughter Julia in England. The originals do not survive, but transcripts were made by Julia and gathered into a single volume. We cannot be certain whether these transcripts are entirely reliable or faithful, but the lengthy letters read fluently; if they have been edited then Julia Howard was able to smooth over any elisions convincingly. The image of Isabella presented in these letters is of a dignified, independent, mature, active woman living in somewhat straitened circumstances.[23]

By October 1771 she had moved from Aix to Beaucaire, in the company of her youngest daughter Julia, aged twenty-one, who became enamoured with a certain 'Monsieur B' (fig. 3). Isabella's apparent lack of interference with this affair excited outrage, and family opposition to this match with an unsuitable Frenchman was so strong that Julia was commanded by her brother the fifth Earl to return to England. Isabella was unrepentant over the matter, having felt all along that Julia was of an age to make up her own mind whether to obey her family's injunctions or persist in the affair; 'I wish your happiness but I cannot dictate to you', she wrote.[24] While respecting Julia's resolution to submit to the prohibition ordered by the family, Isabella repeatedly alluded to the affair in her letters, at one point confessing she was in possession of a letter addressed to Julia from 'Monsieur B'; rather than destroy it she declared, 'I shall lock it up till you order what shall be done with it'.[25] By returning to the affair through such oblique constructions as, 'I will avoid a Subject that may give you pain', or 'a subject that it is better never to named', Isabella was not allowing her daughter to forget the affair; she was testing Julia's determination. But in adopting this tactic she made it harder for the young woman to erase all memory of the attachment, and it is perhaps a telling consequence that Julia remained unmarried until her death in 1849.[26]

Isabella's persistent mention of this unhappy episode was also prompted by her own fury at the reactions of the family which had unsettled her too: she complained of nervous anxiety on receipt of mail from England, 'I am seized with Tremors at the sight of a Packet'; and at one point she cast her suffering in a Shakespearean mode, 'I felt I believe exactly as King Lear did'.[27] The quarrel subsided and in December Isabella moved to Montpellier, where she settled into a cultured milieu attending concerts and soirées.[28] Music was important to her. She

FIGURE 3
A miniature profile portrait of Lady Julia Howard in her later years, J. T. Mitchell, 1809.
THE CASTLE HOWARD COLLECTION

FIGURE 4
A view of the rocks and cascades at Vaucluse in Provence, where Isabella planned to visit in the Spring of 1771. Frontispiece from M. Berenger, *Les Soirées Provençales* (1786).

THE CASTLE HOWARD COLLECTION

owned a harpsichord but seems not to have played it herself; she enjoyed attending and holding concerts, and had a discerning ear. On more than one occasion she copied down 'a scrap of a song' and sent it to England, requesting in return she be sent the latest songs or minuets, 'for I live with so many musical people'.[29]

Through her correspondence we catch a glimpse of an impressive range of skills and activities, confirming that she was of both a practical and intellectual disposition. Shortly after Julia's departure she mentioned how 'my work & my writing go on prodigiously'.[30] Maintaining an extensive network of correspondents, on one occasion she admitted to receiving as many as nine letters from different places in the same post. Her correspondents included family, friends and fellow aristocrats such as the Duchesses of Beaufort, Northumberland, and Portland, confirming that she still retained, at the very least, an epistolary foothold in English society.[31] Her writing also included composing verses and assembling her maxims.[32] Her reading seems to have been intensive, although there is no mention of titles or authors; in 1772 she recorded reading 'more books in one summer than ever I did'.[33] Of the handful of books that survive today that bear her mark of ownership most are, unsurprisingly, French titles, including Berenger's *Soirées Provençales*, 3 vols (1786), with frontispieces depicting local scenery or towns (fig. 4).[34]

Her descriptions of the Provençal landscape reveal a familiarity with the language of the picturesque. The countryside beyond her garden in Montpellier was 'agreeable', and she imagined the terrain further afield to be like Derbyshire, filled with 'rocks, caverns &c'.[35] She relished the view from her window, which ranged down to the sea, and believed it 'so fine that it quite gives one spirits'.[36] Unsurprisingly the mountain ranges around Geneva inspired her even more, 'if fine views & romantick Prospects could contribute my cure wd be complete' she reflected; nor was she content with just un-peopled scenes, from her house in

Cologny she remarked 'the People are getting in their corn & it is a very beautiful sight in this variegated prospect'.[37]

A year earlier, when she had enthused over the castles of Tarascon and Beaucaire, she asserted that 'they merit the best pencil of the artist'.[38] Her detailed descriptions of trees in blossom, and 'romantick prospects', as well as the pleasing compositional qualities of the scenery (trees, cornfields, rocks and the river Rhône), were dismissed by Warren Smith as little more than amateur gushings.[39] In fact her vocabulary and style would suggest a more sophisticated response, moreover one that extended beyond merely verbal description. Thus, among the many 'occupations' reported in her letters, it comes as no surprise to find her engaged in drawing. In December 1771 she announced that she was busy finishing off two views of the chateaux at Beaucaire and Tarascon that straddled the Rhône; at the same time she was taking lessons in drawing from a young French civil servant who specialised in surveying, but this necessitated rising 'before light' as he could not teach her at any other hour. Before long she was pleased with her progress in perspective, complimenting her instructor whose rules were 'very easy & clear'.[40]

Her aptitude for art is not surprising given that she came from a family of talented amateur artists. Her father, William, fourth Lord Byron, had been taught by Peter Tillemans, and had mastered drawing, painting in oil and watercolour, and etching. Isabella's brother, Richard, drew and etched, and she was taught painting and etching by Joseph Goupy.[41] Horace Walpole prized her etchings so highly that he bound thirteen prints, after Rembrandt, Salvator Rosa, Guido Reni and Wencesalus Hollar, into a special album with a dedicated title-page.[42] Her signed works date, mostly, from between 1743 and 1758 when she was married to the fourth Earl of Carlisle. Given that he was a dedicated connoisseur, who assembled during his lifetime an impressive collection of Roman and Venetian paintings (especially works by Pannini and Canaletto), antique sculpture, bronzes, cameos, gems, engravings, and Old Master drawings, he must surely have appreciated and encouraged his wife's artistic pursuits. These appear to have lapsed during the 1760s, and she obviously felt it necessary to be instructed once more on arriving in southern France.

If money permitted she also purchased prints and antiquities. Although she once expressed misgivings about the quality of one of her acquisitions, deferring to her son's authority, it is most unlikely (given her ability to absorb and employ what she had been taught) that she had remained impervious to the art of connoisseurship during her marriage to the fourth Earl.[43] In 1773 Horace Mann reported how Isabella, passing through Florence, had 'showed us so many of her own works and so much practice in pictures, that she was thought very clever in those points here, and gained at the Gallery the reputation of a *connaisseuse*'.[44]

As with her training in accounts and household management, the artistic skills she learnt as a young woman extended to more than just polite pastimes; they constituted real accomplishments, practical disciplines that were put to regular use.

Her life was defined by activity: 'I have all my occupations about me & finding also every material for them here conveniently' she commented in January 1772; later that year she reported 'I have got my Work together & I am beginning my Summer Employs'. Work and books defined her active and intellectual life, and helped combat the loneliness she felt at times.[45]

But her industrious life did not just encompass music, reading, writing and artistic pursuits. She acquired additional intellectual interests and practical skills, these included botany, upholstery, embroidery, cookery, medicine and horticulture, not to mention fluency in French and probably Spanish and Italian. While in Beaucaire she turned her hand to upholstery, working on a set of chairs, but was distressed that some silk that had been sent from England failed to arrive; a local gentleman, was so impressed by her craftsmanship that she gave him one of these chairs; it may be that she learnt this craft from her landlord in Montpellier, whom she described as 'the great Upholsterer here who furnishes all the good houses'.[46] Early the following year she asked for coloured braids to be sent from England for her embroidery work at which she quickly became 'proficient'; she also began making her own gowns.[47]

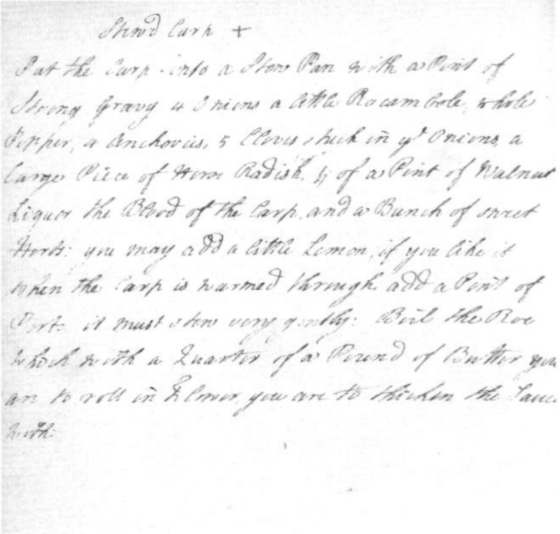
Stew'd Carp +
Put the Carp into a Stew Pan with a Pint of Strong Gravy 4 Onions a little Rocambole, whole Pepper, 2 Anchovies, 5 Cloves stuck in ye Onions a large Piece of Horse Radish, ¼ of a Pint of Walnut Liquor the Blood of the Carp, and a Bunch of sweet Herbs: you may add a little Lemon, if you like it when the Carp is warmed through add a Pint of Port: it must stew very gently: Boil the Roe whole with a Quarter of a Pound of Butter you are to roll in Flower, you are to thicken the Sauce with:

FIGURE 5

A recipe for stewed carp from Isabella's recipe book.

CASTLE HOWARD ARCHIVES

The most remarkable document associated with her is her manuscript recipe book, compiled over the course of her lifetime, and containing more than 200 culinary recipes, medicinal remedies and household tips (figs. 5 & 6).[48] This volume was probably begun while she was mistress of Castle Howard where, in the 1750s, the Kitchen Garden was doubled in acreage and the number of stove-houses for growing exotics increased. She would have had direct access to many of the herbs, fruit and flowers that feature in these recipes, and other ingredients such as mutton, beef and fish would have been available elsewhere on the estate. These recipes were more than just an anthology of fashionable or interesting dishes. The volume was a practical one, something to be consulted when required, especially when she found herself living in reduced circumstances in France. Thus in the autumn of 1771 because she was unable to purchase any locally, she made her own hartshorn jelly, using the recipe from her own book.[49] A few months later, suffering from a stomach complaint, she made her own concoction of orange flower water.[50] Her knowledge of preserving, pickling, baking and cooking is evident from these recipes, as well as her understanding of herbs and medical cures.[51] The book also contains household advice including tips for japanning, making varnish, washing lace, removing the smell of fresh paint from interiors and 'washing old paintings'.[52] Her familiarity with horticulture extended to more than painting flowers, and after arriving in France she refreshed and deepened her knowledge with lessons in botany.[53] Her grasp of agriculture was also sufficiently assured, as was her recollection of the land at Castle Howard, that she even sent the fifth Countess some suggestions for improving one of her fields, recommending that it be sown with buckwheat and corn after further drainage.[54]

Her retired life in France seems to have given her satisfaction. She enjoyed concerts and gatherings, but had to defend her habit of returning home before

Brodsworth Hall

PLATE 1 (LEFT)
Sabine, Mrs Charles Thellusson, and
her son, by Sir Thomas Lawrence, 1804,
oil on canvas.

ENGLISH HERITAGE, BRODSWORTH HALL

PLATE 2 (BELOW)
Georgiana, Mrs Charles Sabine
Thellusson, by Margaret Carpenter,
1850, oil on canvas.

ENGLISH HERITAGE, BRODSWORTH HALL

Brodsworth Hall

PLATE 3 (LEFT)
Sylvia Grant-Dalton in front of
Giuseppe Lazzarini's *Vanity* in 1988.
© LUCINDA LAMBTON

PLATE 4 (BELOW)
Women in Brodsworth Kitchen c. 1910.
ENGLISH HERITAGE, BRODSWORTH

Burton Constable

PLATE 5

The Clifford Children of Tixall Hall,
by Mather Brown, 1806, oil on canvas.

BURTON CONSTABLE HALL

Burton Constable

PLATE 6 (RIGHT)
Prospect of Burton Constable from the
east, Anglo-Dutch school, c. 1690, oil
on canvas.
BURTON CONSTABLE HALL

PLATE 7 (BELOW LEFT)
Lady Chichester with Charles Raleigh
and Arthur, by Claude-Marie Dubufe,
c. 1836–7, oil on canvas.
BURTON CONSTABLE HALL

PLATE 8 (BELOW RIGHT)
Charles Chichester in the uniform of the
14th Regiment of Foot, Irish School,
c.1815, miniature.
CHICHESTER CONSTABLE

Castle Howard

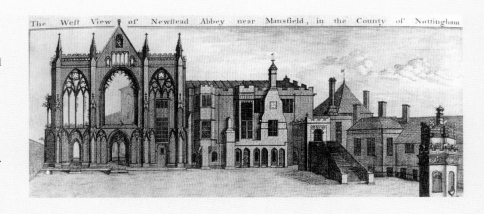

The West View of Newstead Abbey near Mansfield, in the County of Nottingham

Castle Howard

Harewood House

midnight on the occasions when she did dine out. Her view of herself contradicted those of her English critics: 'I hope I derive one advantage from growing old, that I cease to be vain', she wrote on Christmas Eve 1771; she considered her modest regime 'suitable to my Health & Inclination'.[55] Her day was taken up with work and study, weather permitting she would take a daily walk in the countryside, or make longer excursions to Uzes, Vaucluse, Avignon and the sea.[56]

There were difficulties in France; she was accused of poaching a servant from her neighbour, she suffered from fainting fits, and had a fall, spraining her hand badly.[57] In November 1771 there was the first mention of money difficulties that were to plague her for some years. Her bill of credit was refused, and funds from England were held up. Her embarrassment was acute, 'I cannot live with discredit', she raged, and she suspected that her son's London agent, Mr Lavie, was deliberately making life difficult for her.[58] Life on the Continent was cheaper than in England but she recognised that her table was poor in comparison to how it once was, although this was determined as much by her modest lifestyle as by her frugal cook.[59]

From the evidence of her own words, Isabella appears a studious, contented and resourceful woman, prone at times to ill-health, low spirits and loneliness, but far from the scandalous creature berated by her contemporaries in England. Of her own attachment to the self-styled Baron de Wenheim, which caused so much agitation back in England, there is little mention in these letters. He is referred to briefly as having managed her commissions, sent her wine, or acted as her chaperone in public.[60]

Because she was so reticent about the Baron in her own correspondence it is hard to judge the accuracy of the later reports that dismissed him as a fraud. When he eventually joined her in Cologny in 1772 the couple seem to have remained together for the next few years. They journeyed to Italy on the instructions of her doctor, passing through Florence, Rome and Naples.[61] Her finances were evidently dwindling, but her position was not as extreme as that of her brother, the fifth Baron Byron. In the spring of 1772 she had received 'a very kind but melancholy letter' informing her that his profligacy had forced him to auction the picture collection at Newstead, and further financial ruin was to follow. She reacted to this news by observing 'there is a Planet overrules some Familys & blasts every Prospect, I am glad its influence does not circulate to Lord Carlisle'.[62] Little did she know that this malevolent star had also blighted Castle Howard; her son was facing huge debts, and even contemplating moving to Europe in search of a less expensive lifestyle.[63] By 1778 her own affairs had deteriorated sufficiently for the family to dispatch an emissary, the Revd John Warner to detach her from the Baron, settle her financial affairs and bring her back to England from Paris. Warner, whose letters to George Selwyn have formed the basis for our understanding of this colourful episode, was by turns enraged, frustrated and bemused at her behaviour as he struggled to reach an agreement during the winter of 1778-1779.[64] He tried to raise money on her behalf with the banker Sir John Lambert,

FIGURE 6

A recipe for Norfolk punch from Isabella's recipe book.

CASTLE HOWARD ARCHIVES

who had come to her assistance once before in 1771, but she refused to commit herself to returning to England.[65] She reacted with hostility to these attempts to manage her life from a distance, and exchanged fiery letters with Selwyn after he had insulted the Baron.[66] Warner took against the Baron (who had felt it incumbent upon himself to issue a challenge to Selwyn); he likened him to Swift's brutish Yahoos, and relished the humiliating account of how the Baron had apparently been denied an audience with the Young Pretender's wife in Rome because he was not a gentleman.[67] Warner painted a picture of a distressed Isabella, who was 'unhappy and lost', and in 'a deplorable condition'.[68] But the furore subsided, the parties became reconciled, and Warner even escorted the Baron to London in the spring of 1779.[69] Somehow Isabella managed to survive this episode; she was able to stay afloat financially and remain in France, returning to Aix. By 1781 she was said to be preparing to return to England, and Selwyn anticipated 'a fracas' when she eventually arrived home.[70] Once in England she appears to have settled in London and Bath.[71]

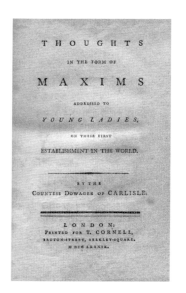

FIGURE 7

Title-page of Isabella's *Thoughts in the Form of Maxims* (1789).
THE CASTLE HOWARD COLLECTION

In reaching an understanding of Isabella's life, it is clear that the words of her contemporaries present only a partial and incomplete view. Her own letters bear witness to a different character, and the documentary material associated with her reveals an intelligent, competent person able to deal with her own affairs. Her financial difficulties appear to have stemmed from an insufficient allowance from England rather than profligacy on her part; nor is there any evidence that the Baron was free with her money. Accustomed to living in some style she was nevertheless able to economise, and draw upon her experience of financial management so ably demonstrated in her housekeeping at Castle Howard; but clearly her funds did not stretch far enough. Upon her return to England, she did not simply vanish, she achieved fame as the 'new noble authoress-dowager', as Walpole termed her, with the publication of her *Maxims* in 1789 (figs. 7 & 8).[72]

The *Maxims* contained more than 400 precepts and sayings intended to assist young women or newly-wed wives on their first entrance into 'the great and critical world'. Written at different periods of her life and based, she claimed in her Introduction, on long 'experience and observation', Isabella felt she could speak authoritatively about a woman's relationship with the 'great and critical world'. The *Maxims* presents the ideal woman as someone who can run an efficient household, manage the accounts, organise servants, keep a good table, and understand something of cooking, medicine and even agriculture. Such responsibilities are not exercised in isolation, they involve delegation and management, skills that must be exercised lightly. The analogy of a fine mechanism (specifically a watch or a timepiece) is used to explain the structure and balance of domestic responsibilities: 'Conceal from the indifferent spectator, the secret springs, which move, regulate, and perfect the arrangement of your household'.[73] This image, not without its aesthetic appeal, emphasises how such a social contract must operate harmoniously in order to ensure a timely and efficient exercise of duty.

Other 'mental acquirements'[74] include the polite arts; the cultured woman is able to play music, write, spell correctly, read, and indulge in a measure of rational and devotional reflection. These accomplishments are supplemented by social skills, the ability to listen and converse appropriately, and the correct observance of feminine decorum.[75] The ideal woman or wife exercises modesty, keeps her counsel, advises discreetly, observes silence, eschews conspicuous behaviour, readily grants forgiveness, and avoids hubris. On the surface these appear prescriptions for the meek. Feminine accomplishment is defined in terms of subordination to social and moral codes, as well as to the commands and needs of a husband: the volume opens with the injunction, 'Habituate yourself to that way of life most agreeable to the person to whom you are united'.

Given our knowledge of Isabella's own life, how are we to read the *Maxims*? As a distillation of her own experience it reads rather like a cautionary tract, urging young women to avoid the difficulties and shocks Isabella had experienced after her separation from her second husband. At the same time, it is hard to accommodate this view of passive womanhood with the active figure who had pursued her independent life on the Continent and resisted all attempts to force her back to England. What is perhaps more significant is how the *Maxims* sits within the eighteenth-century debate on women's education, where instruction in the polite arts was viewed with ambivalence: on the one hand the acquisition of these skills was part of a construction of femininity that idealised the woman as a creature of elegant and refined sensibility; on the other hand these accomplishments were deemed to exacerbate women's tendencies to 'indulge in the most sensationalistic pleasures'.[76]

Isabella's volume is not a catalogue of vacuous aspirations; these accomplishments do not simply constitute a badge of refinement, they are not to be learnt for empty show. As with everything associated with this remarkable woman, the *Maxims* urges the development of a practical, active and reflective self. Many of the sayings are

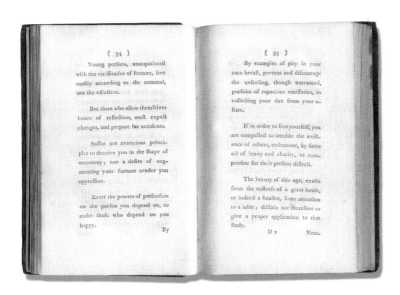

FIGURE 8
Sayings from Isabella's *Thoughts in the Form of Maxims* (1789).
THE CASTLE HOWARD COLLECTION

driven by moralising imperatives such as 'avoid', 'endeavour', 'be cautious', 'suppress' and so on; but there are also more inward recommendations directing her reader to 'adapt', 'question', 'consider', 'contemplate'. She urges her female pupils to use reason, read for instruction, secure their faith, extend their studies, and 'overthrow phantoms'.[77]

Three years after the appearance of the *Maxims* Mary Wollstonecraft published her *Vindication of the Rights of Women* (1792). Wollstonecroft also considered the deleterious effects of education on the female mind, recognising the dangers of 'false refinement', and warning that:

> *Ever restless and anxious their over-excited sensibility not only renders them uncomfortable themselves, but troublesome, to use a soft phrase, to others. All their thoughts turn on things calculated to excite emotion and feeling, when they should reason, their conduct is unstable, and their opinions are wavering – not the wavering produced by deliberation or progressive views, but by contradictory emotions.*[78]

Isabella's *Maxims*, with its emphasis upon self-scrutiny, encouraged deliberation and progressive views. Her volume was not a sustained polemic like the *Vindication* but within its lighter form – part proverbial, part aphoristic – Isabella proffered a balance between reason and imagination. Thus she recommended reading both for instruction and for pleasure in two consecutive maxims:

> *Romances, of a moral nature, may not prove unuseful, in their effects on a mind fatigued by unavoidable application.*

> *An excessive love of romance will make you expect to lead the life of one, and will place common cares too low in your estimation for you to attend to them.*[79]

Wollstonecraft had feared how 'Novels, music, poetry and gallantry, all tend to make women the creatures of sensation'. While Isabella cautioned against the 'overstretched sensibility' she saw no contradiction in recognising the value of feeding the imagination.

How finally should Isabella be judged? Her accomplishments were diverse, she held intellectual and practical pursuits in equal esteem, although the most significant omission from her personal repertoire is any strong sense of motherhood. One way in which to understand her is to return to the portraits by Dahl and Gainsborough. As a painter, an etcher, an upholsterer, and someone used to dealing with herbs, medicines, and tinctures, as well as flowers, vegetables, meat and fish, in the course of her lifetime her hands would have changed from those smooth tapering fingers seen in the Dahl portrait. Her hands and fingernails would have shown signs of her practical life: paint, ink, soil, juices and other markings; the skin may well have grown coarse from working with needles and other implements. Her hands are not depicted in the Gainsborough portrait and one is left wondering just how manicured and elegant they really were.

Her reply in verse to Mrs Greville's 'A Prayer for Indifference', (according to Roger Lonsdale the 'most celebrated poem by a woman in the period'), reveals a desire to challenge and champion all aspects of life – its pleasures and its shocks.

Her appetite for life is unmistakable, 'Give me, whatever I possess,/To know and feel it all', she proclaimed. Half measures held no appeal for her:

It never shall be my desire
To bear a heart unmoved;
To feel by halves the generous fire,
Or be but half beloved

Let me drink deep the dangerous cup,
In hopes the prize to gain;
Nor tamely give the pleasure up,
Nor fear to share the pain.[80]

There is an unmistakable Byronic foretaste in these words, and this points to one final intriguing dimension to this extraordinarily accomplished and intelligent woman: what might be termed the world of historical near-misses.

In 1771 while residing in Beaucaire she described an entertaining evening in the company of 'the Messrs. de Sade'. A few weeks later she recorded 'Monr. de Sade came to dine with me yesterday & the Abbé'.[81] We do not know who exactly this Monsieur de Sade was, although earlier in the year she had mentioned a Baron de Sade who she had described as an old man.[82] The Abbé, who she referred to as 'my friend', was the Abbé de Sade, author of a life of Petrarch, and uncle to the infamous Marquis de Sade, who had lived with his uncle as a young boy. At one point Isabella even made plans for an expedition to Avignon to see the tomb of Laura, Petrarch's great beloved, from whom the de Sades were descended. In the autumn of 1771 the Marquis de Sade had returned to the family chateau at La Coste, a few miles from Beaucaire, where he was rehearsing with his troupe of actors; within six months he would journey to Marseilles to seek his grim and violent forms of pleasure, before returning to La Coste with a warrant issued for his arrest.[83] We shall never know if Isabella met the thirty-one-year-old Marquis in the autumn of 1771, just as we shall never know if some months later, when living on the outskirts of Geneva, she did eventually call on Voltaire, after putting off her visit the first time.[84] What these two episodes indicate is that Isabella was not living in isolation, even though she felt so remote that she claimed to her daughter, 'It is like writing from the Antipodes to a world like yours'.[85] Her regular correspondence, her encounters with French society, and with the multitude of English travellers (even though she did affect to dislike them),[86] show how integrated she was in the world of culture and letters.

The most extraordinary instance of historical chance is connected with her time in Switzerland, where she arrived in May 1772, renting a villa at Cologny, on the southern shore of Lake Geneva. That summer she witnessed 'the most violent storm I ever saw or heard of'; in addition to thunder, lightening, wind, and hail, the rain forced itself 'into every room in rivers'. The following morning dozens of dead birds littered her garden, struck down in the storm.[87] In itself, this account of a summer Alpine storm is unremarkable apart from its ferocity. What is more intriguing is how exactly forty-four years later, in May 1816, her great nephew,

Lord Byron would arrive in Geneva, escaping from scandal and notoriety in England. Shortly afterwards he took a villa at Cologny above the shores of the lake in the company of his doctor John Polidori. His neighbours, staying in a more modest house five minutes walk away, were Percy Shelley and Mary Godwin (daughter of Mary Wollstonecraft). This remarkable quartet also witnessed several summer storms, which Mary Godwin claimed were 'grander and more terrific than I have ever seen before'. In late May she recorded how 'One night we enjoyed a finer storm than I had ever before beheld'.[88] This violent natural event would in time be indirectly responsible for one of the greatest works of romantic fiction, Mary Shelley's *Frankenstein*, published in 1818. Spawned from nocturnal discussions about the spiritual and the rational, in the company of Byron, Shelley and Polidori, this novel was also concerned with the balance between reason and imagination, and the limits of the practical and the intellectual. Set in the fictional year of '17—', at one point the central character Frankenstein returns to Geneva where he too witnesses a great storm; after rowing across the lake, he spies in the gloom a figure by the shore, the creature he had fashioned. During the summer of 1816 one other figure also rowed across Lake Geneva, Lord Byron, perhaps he too sensed another presence, an ancestral spirit haunting the vicinity of Cologny.[89]

I am grateful to the Hon Simon Howard and Philip Howard for permission to reproduce images at Castle Howard and Naworth Castle respectively. My thanks also to Alison Brisby, Dr Ruth Larsen, Dr David Griffiths, Peter Smith Photography, and Gordon Smith of the University of York Photographic Department.

1 As told in Smith, W.H., *Originals Abroad, The Foreign Careers of Some Eighteenth-Century Britons* (New Haven, 1952), pp. 97-112. Smith's principal source material comes from Jesse, J.H., *George Selwyn and His Contemporaries*, (London 1843-44, 4 vols), hereafter referred to as Jesse, which reprints many of the letters sent from France by Revd John Warner on his mission to bring Isabella home to England in 1779-80; there is also a selection of letters from Isabella from an earlier period in 1771. This material is supplemented by Stuart, Lady Louisa, *Notes on George Selwyn*, W.S. Lewis (ed.), (New York, 1928), pp. 46-9.

2 The Castle Howard Archives contain a great deal of material relating to Isabella that was not consulted by Smith in his account of her life. This includes the copy letter book of her correspondence with her daughter Julia Howard, 1771-1773 (J13/1/3); *My Book of Receipts* (J13/1/4); *An Abstract of the House Accounts*, 1744-1755 (H1/1/4); her deed of separation from her second husband Sir William Musgrave in 1769 (J13/2/1); among the papers of her son, the fifth Earl, is correspondence from Musgrave (J14/1/1-13); and papers relating to Isabella's financial affairs (J14/13-17).

3 For further background on the Byrons and Newstead see, Beckett, J., *Byron and Newstead: The Aristocrat and the Abbey* (Delaware, 2002), and Jackson-Stops, G., 'Newstead Abbey', *Country Life*, clv (9 May and 16 May, 1974), pp. 1122-5, 1190-3.

4 Halsband R. (ed.), *The Complete Letters of Lady Mary Wortley Montagu*, (Oxford, 1965-7, 3 vols), ii, 311.

5 *An Abstract of the House Accounts*, 1744-1755 (H1/1/4), p.1. Hereafter referred to as *Abstract*.

6 *Abstract*, pp. 6, 7, 21, 29, 35, 115.

7 *Abstract*, p. 63.

8 *Abstract*, pp. 53, 89.

9 *Abstract*, pp. 65, 76, and 15-16.

10 *Thoughts in the Form of Maxims* (London, 1789), p. 33. Hereafter referred to as *Maxims*.

11 *The Complete Letters*, iii, 184.

12 Conway to Walpole, 27 August 1758, W.S. Lewis et al (eds.) *Horace Walpole's Correspondence*, (New Haven, 1937-83, 48 vols), xxxvii, 561. Hereafter abbreviated to *HWC*.

13 Walpole to George Montagu, 17 November 1759, *HWC*, ix, 260.

14 *The Letters and Journals of Lady Mary Coke*, (Edinburgh, 1889-96, 4 vols), i, 181-82, n. 4. Hereafter referred to as *Coke*.

15 Waterhouse, E., *Gainsborough* (London, 1958), no. 119, p. 58. Waterhouse dates the painting to soon after 1760.

16 MS volume of reminiscences entitled *Melange*, c. 1820, (J14/65/5), pp. 29-30.

17 John Ingamells states the marriage was dissolved within two years, *A Dictionary of British and Irish Travellers in Italy 1701-1800* (New Haven, 1997), p. 181; in 1768 George Selwyn called on Musgrave in London but referred to the premises as belonging to Isabella, Roscoe, E.S. and H. Clergue, *George Selwyn, His Letters and His Life* (London, 1899), pp. 48, 60; in February 1769 Lady Mary Coke reported that 'Ly Carlisle was going to be separated from Sir William Musgrave', *Coke*, iii, 20; the eventual deed of separation was not drawn up until a year later, and is dated 15 March 1769 (J13/2/1).

18 Horace Walpole to Lord Hertford, 3 September 1765, *HWC*, xxxv, 317. *Coke*, i, 202, 209-10; ii, 236, 256, 286. Her presence in London is also corroborated by Selwyn, see above note 17. Smith, *Originals Abroad*, p. 102, places her in Florence but this is likely to be a mistake, as the letter that he refers to, from Sir Horace Mann to Horace Walpole, is in fact dated 24 November 1772, *HWC*, xxiii, 447; however Ingamells accepts this, *Dictionary*, pp.181-82. What is certain is that Isabella's son, the fifth Earl, was in Italy in 1768, and his correspondence makes no mention of either being accompanied by his mother or of meeting her.

19 *Coke*, iii, 292, 338, 457.

20 *Coke*, iii, 479.

21 Her male admirers on the other hand had declared her handsome and witty, see note 12 above; although Walpole had at one point cast aspersions on her morality with an anecdote in a letter to George Montagu in January 1760. Describing how Lord Temple was importuning George II for the Order of the Garter (following the vacancy in the Order left by the death of the fourth Earl of Carlisle), Walpole observed, 'he went, and at once asked for my Lord Carlisle's Garter – if he would have been contented to ask first for my Lady Carlisle's garter, I don't doubt he would have obtained it', *HWC*, ix, 271. Lady Mary Coke's severity is perhaps easy to explain given that she was perceived as a rival widow for the affections of Walpole, see Walpole to Conway, 2 September 1758, *HWC*, xxxviii, 563. Perhaps the most dispassionate female judgement about Isabella comes from Madame Du Deffand, who seems to have considered her something of a bore, incapable of conversation that was either interesting or shocking; in 1778 she remarked, 'ses visites me fatiguent, heureusement elles sont rares', *HWC*, vii, 50-51, 61.

22 Letter to George Selwyn, *Jesse*, iv, 211.

23 *Letterbook* (J13/1/3), containing forty-eight transcribed letters, dated between 25 October 1771 and 6 January 1773. Hereafter abbreviated to LBK.

24 *LBK*, Letter 1, 25 October 1771. This was not the first time that her behaviour with regard to settling her children had occasioned disapproval, see above, note 19.

25 *LBK*, Letter 19, 27 January; see also Letter 4, n.d.

26 *LBK*, Letters 14, 24 December [1771]; 22, 10 February 1772; see also Letters 13, n.d., and 18, 8 January 1772.

27 *LBK*, Letters 1, 25 October 1771; 9, 29 November 1771.

28 'I like my situation exceedingly & my society', she wrote, *LBK*, Letter 14, 24 December 1771.

29 *LBK*, Letters 13, n.d.; 15, 13 January 1772; 18, 8 January 1772; 21, 10 January 1772; 22, 10 February 1772; 26, 11 March 1772; 34, 24 May 1772; 44, 17 August 1772. In England she was renowned for her love of concerts, in 1758, George Montagu had reported 'a great concert at my Lady Carlisle's', Montagu to Horace Walpole, 4 May 1758, *HWC*, ix, 219.

30 *LBK*, Letter 4, 10 November 1771.

31 *LBK*, Letter 48, 14 August 1772.

32 *LBK*, Letter 15, 13 January 1772. When the Revd Warner met Isabella in Paris in December 1778, he reported to George Selwyn how she 'read me a moral essay of her own composition, in the shape of maxims', evidence that she was assembling her thoughts long before publication in 1789, *Jesse*, iii, 358-9. Her poem 'Answer to Mrs Greville's Ode for Indifference' is printed in *Jesse*, iii, 319-20, although Jesse attributes it to Isabella's daughter-in-law Caroline, fifth Countess of Carlisle. Lady Louisa Stuart disputes this, and assigns the composition to Isabella, *Notes on George Selwyn*, p. 46. See also Lonsdale, R., (ed.), *Eighteenth-Century Women Poets* (Oxford, 1989), under Frances Greville, pp. 190-4.

33 *LBK*, Letter 41, n.d.

34 Eight titles bearing her signature survive in the library at Castle Howard. Five are French volumes, and two are Spanish including an edition of *Don Quixote*; the lone English title is a set of Alexander Pope's works.

35 *LBK*, Letters 14, 24 December 1771; 20, n.d.

36 *LBK*, Letters 16, 16 December 1771; 21, 10 January 1772.

37 *LBK*, Letters 35, 1 June 1772; 40, 13 July 1772.

38 Letter to Selwyn, *Jesse*, iv, 123.

39 Letters to Selwyn and Caroline, Countess of Carlisle, *Jesse*, IV, 68, 107, 158. Smith claimed she was no genius with words, *Originals Abroad*, p. 98.

40 *LBK*, Letters 13, n.d.; 14, 24 December 1771; 15, 13 January 1772; 20, n.d.; 21, 10 January 1772.

41 Sloan, K., *A Noble Art, Amateur Artists and Drawing Masters, c.1600-1800*, exh. cat. (London, 2000), pp. 88, 221-3.

42 Sloan, *Noble Art*, p. 223. The album is described in Hazen, A. T., *A Catalogue of Horace Walpole's Library*, (New Haven, 1969), iii, no. 3588, pp. 149-150; the album is located in the Lewis Walpole Library, Yale University, Farmington, CT. Walpole referred to Isabella as the widow of the fourth Earl who 'paints flowers in water-colours, very neatly, and etches after drawings, *Anecdotes of Painting*, Hilles and Dahglian (eds.), (New Haven, 1937), v, p. 229.

43 *LBK*, Letters 20, n.d.; 26, 11 March 1772.

44 Horace Mann to Walpole, 30 January 1773, *HWC*, xxiii, 457.

45 *LBK*, Letters 15, 13 January 1772; 33, 10 May 1772; 39, 6 July 1772

46 *LBK*, Letters 9, 29 November 1771; 10, 4 December 1771; 11, 6 December 1771; 16, 16 December 1771.

47 *LBK*, Letters 23, February 1772; 26, 11 March 1772; 29, 25 March 1772; 32, 29 April 1772; 40, 13 July 1772.

48 *My Book of Receipts* (J13/1/4). Hereafter *Receipts*.

49 *LBK*, Letter 6, 17 November 1771; *Receipts*, p. 137.

50 *LBK*, Letter 27, 25 March 1772; *Receipts*, p. 140.

51 These included, A Receipt for an Ague (p. 1), A Cure for a Sore Throat (p. 2), A Remedy for disorders of the Spirits (p. 3), A Receipt for a Cold (p. 4), Heart Burn Lozenges (p. 11), Lady Berkeley's Mouth Water (p. 12), A Receipt for Hooping Cough (p. 29), In case of being Poisoned by Mushrooms, (p. 60), and numerous other remedies.

52 *Receipts*, pp. 41, 241, 242, 252, 255.

53 *LBK*, Letters 13, [December 1771]; 26, 11 March 1772.

54 *LBK*, Letter 12, 10 December 1771.

55 *LBK*, Letters 14, 24 December 1771; 20, n.d.

56 Letters to Selwyn, *Jesse*, iv, 122, 209; *LBK*, Letter 18, 8 January 1772.

57 *LBK*, Letters 15, 13 January 1772; 18, 8 January 1772; 19, 27 January 1772.

58 *LBK*, Letters 7, 22 November 1771; 8, 25 November 1771; 10, 4 December 1771.

59 Letter to Selwyn, *Jesse*, iv, 323-324; *LBK*, Letters 34, 24 May 1772; 35, 1 June 1772.

60 *LBK*, Letters, 28, 29 March 1772; 32, 29 April 1772; 34, 24 May 1772; 39, 6 July 1772.

61 *LBK*, Letter 44, 17 August 1772; Ingamells, *Dictionary*, pp. 181-82.

62 *LBK*, Letter 25, 6 March 1772.

63 Fifth Earl correspondence with Selwyn, *Jesse*, iii, 51, 60-1, 67, 92-7, 107-9, 129-31, 136, 160-2.

64 Reprinted in *Jesse*, vols iii and iv.

65 *Jesse*, iii, 360-366; iv, 18; for Lambert's assistance earlier see *LBK*, Letter 11, 6 December 1771.

66 *Jesse*, iii, 380-387.

67 *Jesse*, iii, 392.

68 *Jesse*, iii, 387, iv, 31.

69 *Jesse*, iv, 67.

70 Horace Walpole to Thomas Walpole, 25 March 1781, *HWC*, xxxvi, 193; Roscoe and Clergue, *George Selwyn*, p. 152.

71 Smith, *Originals Abroad*, p. 112; among the papers of her son the fifth Earl is a document relating to furnishings for a house in Bath, document addressed to John Smith, dated 9 July 1787 (J14/17); she also had kept a house in London, which was let during her absence, *LBK*, Letter 10, 4 December [1771]; this may have been the means by which she was able to raise money in the winter of 1778-79.

72 Walpole to Lady Ossory, 26 December 1789, *HWC*, xxxiv, 89. A second edition of the *Maxims* was published in London in 1790, and a further edition in the same year with a Dublin imprint.

73 *Maxims*, p. 32. Her familiarity with timepieces was more than just metaphorical, whilst in Cologny she twice mentioned how she could obtain quality watches from Mr de Falger the 'famous watchmaker', *LBK*, Letters, 44, 17 August 1772; 45, 24 August 1772.

74 *Maxims*, p. 130.

75 The section on social behaviour places great stress on polite listening and avoiding interruption, see especially *Maxims*, p. 71. In 1771 Isabella had reported an instance of interrupted conversation and its attendant 'Inquietude', *LBK*, Letter 9, 29 November 1771.

76 The phrase is taken from Bermingham, A., *Learning to Draw, Studies in the Cultural History of a Polite and Useful Art* (New Haven, 2000), p. 191. Her account of women's accomplishments informs much this discussion.

77 *Maxims*, pp. 98-102.

78 Wollstonecraft, M., *Vindication of the Rights of Women* (Harmondsworth, 1983), p. 152.

79 *Maxims*, pp. 102-3.

80 For Mrs Greville and her 'Prayer', see Lonsdale ed., *Eighteenth-Century Women Poets*, pp. 190-4. Isabella's reply is reprinted in *Jesse*, iii, 319-20.

81 *LBK*, Letters 5, 15 November 1771; 12, 10 December 1771.

82 Letter to Selwyn, *Jesse*, iv, 125-126.

83 For de Sade see, Lily, G., *The Marquis de Sade, A Biography* (New York, 1961), ch. 2; and also Thomas, D., *The Marquis de Sade* (London, 1993), pp. 17-22, 35-8, 40-2, 49, 69-72, 98-103, 107-12.

84 *LBK*, Letter 34, 24 May 1772.

85 *LBK*, Letter 25, 6 March 1772.

86 *LBK*, Letter 39, 6 July 1772.

87 *LBK*, Letter 41, n.d., but probably July 1772; the storm was followed by such excessive heat that it caused the ink in her pen to coagulate.

88 Bennett, B. T. (ed.), *The Letters of Mary Wollstonecraft Shelley*, (Baltimore, 1980-1988, 3 vols), i, 20. For accounts of that Genevan summer see: Holmes, R., *Shelley, The Pursuit* (London, 1974), ch. 13; Seymour, M., *Mary Shelley* (London, 2000), ch. 11.

89 Shelley, M., *Frankenstein*, M. Butler (ed.), (Oxford, 1994), pp. 55-57. For Byron's rowing trip, made with Shelley, see MacCarthy, F., *Byron, Life and Legend* (London, 2002), pp. 290-3; also Marchand L. (ed.), *Byron's Letters and Journals*, (London, 1973-1982, 12 vols), v, 80-7.

Frances Ball
d.1761

Elizabeth Dawes
d.1764

m.1

Edwin Lascelles
1712–1795

m.2

Jane Colman
1731/2–1813

Edward Lascelles
1st Earl
1740–1820

m.

Anne Chaloner
1st Countess
1742/3–1805

Mary Chaloner
c.1743–1803

Dorothy Seymour Fleming
d.1818

Jane Fleming
1755–1824

Henrietta Sebright
2nd Countess
1770–1840

m.

Henry Lascelles
2nd Earl
1767–1841

Frances Lascelles
1762–1817

Mary Lascelles
1775–1831

George Canning
1770–1827

m.

Joan Scott
1776–1837

Louisa Thynne
3rd Countess
1801–1859

m.

Henry Lascelles
3rd Earl
1797–1857

Harriet Lascelles
1802–1889

Ulick de Burgh
14th Earl &
1st Marquess
of Clanricarde

The Clanricarde Inheritance

m.

Harriet Canning
1804–76

Charles Earl Canning
1812–1862

m.

Charlotte Stuart
1817–1861

Louisa Stuart
1818–1891

Mary Meade
1842–1866

Henry Thynne Lascelles
4th Earl
1824–1892

m.

Elizabeth de Burgh
4th Countess
1826–1854

Emily de Burgh
1828–1912

Hubert George de Burgh
15th Earl &
2nd Marquess
of Clanricarde
1832–1916

Constance Lascelles
1852–1932

Henry Ulick Lascelles
5th Earl
1846–1929

m.

Florence Bridgeman
5th Countess
1859–1943

King George V
1865–1936

m.

Queen Mary
1867–1953

Henry George Charles Lascelles
6th Earl
1882–1947

m.

HRH Princess Mary The Princess Royal
6th Countess
1897–1965

Marion Stein
b.1926

m.1

George Henry Hubert Lascelles
7th Earl
b.1923

m.2

Patricia Tuckwell
7th Countess
b.1926

Some Lascelles Ladies

KAREN LYNCH

In all families there are strong characters whose stories are passed from generation to generation. The Lascelles family of Harewood House, near Leeds in Yorkshire, is no exception. However, history has tended to highlight the lives and achievements of the male of the species, with the female relegated to the background. This essay will introduce some of the women who play a part in the history of Harewood. The family tree opposite will help illustrate the different generations of the family.

Harewood House was commissioned by Edwin Lascelles in 1759 to replace Gawthorpe Hall, a medieval manor house that had become unfashionable in an age when the neo-classical ruled. Edwin chose as his architect John Carr of York, and the interiors were designed by Robert Adam with furniture by Thomas Chippendale. Gawthorpe Hall, which stood close to the present stable block at Harewood, was demolished when the new house was ready for the family in 1771. Lancelot 'Capability' Brown, and other leading designers of the day landscaped the grounds. Two earlier buildings were retained as eyecatchers in the landscape and to provide echoes of the past: Harewood Castle and All Saints Church both remain today within the park at Harewood and they introduce two powerful women who, whilst not part of the Lascelles story, shaped part of the estate we see today.

William de Aldburgh, son of the builder of Harewood Castle, died in 1391 and the Harewood estate passed to his two daughters, Elizabeth and Sibyl. These sisters and their husbands, Sir Richard Redman and Sir William Ryther respectively, seem to have reached an unusual agreement to share the castle and to thus avoid breaking up the estate. The sisters were also responsible for the construction of a new church at Harewood on the site of an earlier building. Although there have been many changes over the last six centuries the church is still home to magnificent alabaster monuments to the heiresses and their husbands (fig. 1).

Returning to the Lascelles family of Harewood the story begins with Henry Lascelles, a merchant who had amassed a substantial fortune through trading with the West Indies. The family seat was Stank Hall, a modest house near

53

FIGURE 1

Alabaster tomb from All Saints'
Church, Harewood.

Northallerton. Henry purchased the Harewood and Gawthorpe estates in 1738 but there is no evidence that he spent much time in Yorkshire, preferring his London home. By 1746 Henry's eldest son, Edwin Lascelles, was running the estate and early the following year Edwin married Elizabeth Dawes, a wealthy Yorkshire heiress. Little is known about Elizabeth other than that she had two sons who both died in their infancy and that she died in 1764 at Bath, where she was possibly taking the waters for her health. Six years later Edwin Lascelles remarried. His bride was Jane Fleming (née Colman) the widow of Sir John Fleming, and she chose to retain her title of Lady Fleming rather than be known as plain Mrs Lascelles. Lady Fleming arrived at Harewood just as work on the new house was nearing completion although visitors in 1771 and 1773 noted that the interiors were far from complete.[1] Her presence at Harewood was welcomed in a poem:

A hill so charming, & a vale so sweet,
Wanted, Eliza, to make all complete!
The great default the God of Love perceives,
And to adorn the whole fair Fleming gives![2]

As a Member of Parliament Edwin spent much of the year in London, but both he and Lady Fleming wrote frequent letters to the steward at Harewood to give instructions. Although there is no evidence of how great a part Lady Fleming played in the furnishing and decoration of the house, she was actively involved in planning the gardens and plantations that embellished the mansion. Lady Fleming was particularly involved with a new plantation north of the house and commissioned a number of romantic structures. She was also very fond of birds and as well as caged birds in the house, she had a menagerie, where she and her friends could take tea and feed the ornamental pheasants.

Lady Fleming brought with her to Harewood her two daughters, Jane and Seymour Dorothy. Portraits at Harewood show these two ladies to be great beauties, but they had a further attraction – a huge fortune bequeathed to them by their late father. Press reports were clearly as imprecise as they can be today and the exact sums involved varied hugely from one account to the next. A Leeds newspaper announced the marriage in 1775 of Seymour Dorothy to Sir Richard Worsley of Appuldurcombe and described her as 'a Lady of the finest accomplishments, with a fortune of 100,000l'.[3] Seymour Dorothy was painted by Sir Joshua Reynolds shortly after her marriage. She is portrayed in the uniform of her husband's regiment, the Hampshire Militia; there was a trend at this date for aristocratic women to express their patriotism by dressing in riding habits adapted from military uniforms (plate 13). Lady Worsley appears to have been the instigator of a number of pranks at Harewood and one Christmas she was not to be beaten when her step-father refused her permission to take his carriage into Leeds. Aided and abetted by two friends Lady Worsley took the carthorses and rode into Leeds. A contemporary letter describes the events of the evening:

They stopt at one of the Inns and ordered the waiter to show them into such a room
which he told them he could not do, as it was kept for the officers of the militia and

their colours etc. were there. But they were determined to go in and took the pokers and broke open the door, then they heated them red hot and pop'd them into the colours which set them in a blaze. How do you think they quenched the flame their own fair selves had caused? They did not call water! water!, it was more at hand. They fairly —— —— it out … this is a specimen of the wit and courage of the belles of Harewood.[4]

Events of 1782 would bring Lady Worsley to national prominence. In that year the Worsleys went to court in one of the most sensational 'criminal conversation' (i.e. adultery) cases of the century. Sir Richard sued Captain Bisset, an officer in his regiment, for eloping with Lady Worsley, and sought damages of £20,000. But the judge awarded only one shilling on hearing that Sir Richard had encouraged Bisset to spy on his naked wife when she was in a bathhouse. The affair was celebrated in a number of satirical prints, including one with the caption:

Sir Richard Worse-than-sly
Exposing his wife's bottom − o fye![5]

The most scandalous part of the proceedings was that Lady Worsley called a number of gentlemen to court to swear that they had been her lovers. Horace Walpole wrote to a friend about the scandal:

she summoned thirty four men of the first quality to depose to having received her favours, and one of them, a Duke's son, to having bestowed an additional one on her.[6]

Walpole was hinting that Lady Worsley had been infected with a venereal disease and the Duke's son, the Marquess of Graham, was questioned in court on this subject. After the case Lady Worsley did as most disgraced aristocrats did when embroiled in scandal, she moved to the Continent, although she was sad to leave her only son. Ostracized by her mother and sister she was accepted back into the family only after the death of Sir Richard in 1805. As the Worsley's son had not survived to adulthood, Lady Worsley's marriage settlement was returned to her by Sir Richard's executors. The artist and diarist Joseph Farington noted the jaundiced view that this new wealth was 'supposed to have caused a restoration of affections and intimacy between her and her sister Lady Harrington'.[7] Soon after the death of her first husband Lady Worsley, who by now had the permission of the King to call herself Lady Fleming, married a Frenchman and spent the rest of her life living between London and Paris.

Meanwhile, Lady Worsley's sister, Jane, had married Charles, third Earl of Harrington in 1779 (plate 14). Jane's fortune was immediately put to use in settling the debts of the previous generation of Harringtons. Jane was considered a great beauty and was listed as one of the best-dressed ladies in London by a newspaper; she was in illustrious company as the list also featured HRH the Duchess of Cumberland and Georgiana, Duchess of Devonshire.[8] Jane seems to have lived a life free from the scandal that surrounded her sister and became an intimate of Queen Charlotte as one of her Ladies of the Bedchamber. She was a great hostess and her tea parties were famed throughout London.

Edwin Lascelles, by now Lord Harewood, died without issue in 1795 and his

FIGURE 2

Mrs. Hale, by Sir Joshua Reynolds,
c. 1762-64, oil on canvas.

wealth and estates passed to his cousin Edward Lascelles although his title became extinct. Edward immediately moved to Harewood with his wife Ann, née Chaloner, and in the following year the King revived the title Baron Harewood for him. The family archive reveals little about Ann Chaloner other than that she was a popular chatelaine. The first guidebook to Harewood House tells us that the portrait of Ann by Sir Joshua Reynolds features her in the character of *Penseroso* from a poem by John Milton popular at that time.[9] Ann's sister Mary was married to General John Hale, a hero of the war with America who served with General Wolfe at Quebec. Her portrait by Reynolds shows her in the character of Euphrosyne, also from a Milton poem, and when it was issued as a print is was captioned *L'Allegro* (fig. 2).[10] It would seem that Ann was the quiet sister and Mary the more vibrant of the two. Mary certainly lived up to her name – she was 'hale' enough to produce twenty-one children, including two sets of twins. A descendant later described her as:

> … *a woman of great originality and high integrity. Her husband's means being scanty she educated her numerous family herself. She was indeed a peerless woman of her time, virtuous, talented and charming, the delight of all around her.*[11]

Ann, Lady Harewood, had four children, two sons and two daughters. The youngest child, Mary Ann was born in 1775 and was involved in a minor scandal in 1801 when she eloped with Richard York, son of a wealthy Leeds merchant (fig. 3). Mary Hale wrote to a relative with the latest news:

> *At present indeed the whole family of Harewood and their relatives have had enough to talk about and a thousand "I daresays" and "I wonders" etc. etc., for lo! and behold, Miss Lascelles … has thought proper to elope with a young man who was either enamoured with her extensive person, or more probably with her prospective fortune … Miss Lascelles left her Father's house very early in the morning, and herself opened the door into the street with a bundle of cloathes under her arm, and was married … I hear Lord and Lady Harewood are more composed than they were, and for my part I think it may be all for the best, for she was certainly a great Plague to them all, and as a husband has long been her aim, she may in future be more placid.*[12]

Lord and Lady Harewood did eventually accept the match and the Yorks settled not far from Harewood, at Wighill Park, near Tadcaster.

Edward, Lord Harewood was created an earl in 1812 and his eldest son took the courtesy title of Viscount Lascelles. The first Earl died in 1820 and as his eldest son had predeceased him the title went to Henry, his second son. Henry had married Henrietta Saunders Sebright in 1794. Queen Charlotte was unsure about the match:

> The younger Lascelles, alias Cupid, is to marry Miss Sebright. The gay Lothario is to wed the sedate and retired wife; how they will suit, time will shew; for beauty there is none, nor fortune on the female side … She has been well educated; as I hear, is possessed of many talents, and has behaved with great attention to her mother.[13]

Despite the Queen's reservations Henry and Henrietta appear to have flourished and produced a large family of eight sons and four daughters. Henrietta came from a mildly eccentric family and there are many accounts of her brother's unusual behaviour. Sir John Saunders Sebright was encountered at a social event in 1830 by John Cam Hobhouse, who wrote in his memoirs:

> Sir J Sebright was of the party, and told us of his skill in instructing puppies. He can make them extract cube roots. He does it by the eye entirely. One of Sir John Sebright's daughters has invented an expeditious mode of extracting cubes, which he showed me. What between his dogs and his daughters, his family must be an ingenious circle![14]

Some years earlier the Duke of Rutland had visited Harewood and found Henrietta in 'considerable anxiety' as her brother had just been imprisoned for shooting his own groom.[15] Henrietta's unconventional family entertained prominent figures from the worlds of art and science at their home at Beechwood Park, Hertfordshire, and she was no doubt influenced by these people, becoming a talented artist and also experimenting very successfully with engraving her own works.

Henrietta's eldest daughter Harriet, who was born in 1802, inherited her talent and curiosity. There is a painting at Harewood of the four daughters of the second Earl and it is Harriet who is most striking as she carries a prop – her sketchbook (plate 15). Many volumes of Harriet's drawings survive amongst her husband's family papers as well as a number of drawings at Harewood (fig. 4).[16] The name of Harriet's drawing master has not been discovered but she would have grown up at Harewood and at the family's London home surrounded by the inspirational collection of watercolours by J.M.W. Turner, Thomas Girtin and others collected by her uncle, Edward, Viscount Lascelles. But Harriet did not restrict herself to the gentle art of drawing. She was also a keen natural philosopher (the term scientist was not then in use) and conducted many experiments at Harewood. In this she was guided by two of the greatest chemists in London at this time – Sir Humphry Davy and Dr William Hyde Wollaston. Both men visited Harewood and corresponded with Harriet to discuss her work. Davy sent her drawings of strata in rock and a piece of wire gauze – he had been staying at Harewood immediately before his announcement of the use of wire gauze in the safety lamp that revolutionized life in the mining industry. Wollaston sent her samples of metal wrapped in paper and inscribed 'For the renowned chemist of Harewood from her

most obsequious slave.'[17] He also made her a gift of a hydrometer to measure specific gravity and when she was frustrated with her work he wrote:

I really cannot allow you to accuse yourself either of stupidity or ignorance any more than want of industry, for I may truly say that your experiments are well devised and your inferences very correct with the exception of a little oversight arising from inexperience.[18]

In 1825 Harriet married the Earl of Sheffield and settled at Sheffield Place, his family seat in Sussex. She continued to sketch at home and on tours of Britain and the continent but there is no evidence that she further developed her interest in science.

Many generations of the family produced an event worthy of gossip and amongst Harriet's siblings there would be two affairs discussed in family letters. Harriet's sister Emma married Edward Portman, later Baron Portman of Bryanston, in 1827. When Princess Victoria visited Harewood in 1835 she was much taken with Emma and her young daughter Ella, and as soon as she became Queen she wrote to invite Lady Portman to become a Lady of the Bedchamber. Lady Portman attended Queen Victoria at the Coronation in 1837 but only two years later there was a sudden drop in the Queen's popularity as news of the 'Flora Hastings' affair reached the public. Lady Flora Hastings was unmarried and a Lady in Waiting to the Queen. Ladies of the Court, including Lady Portman, reported to the Queen their belief that Lady Flora was pregnant and the Queen, despite Lady Flora Hastings' declarations of innocence, believed the story. Lady Flora was forced to submit to a medical examination and it found that she was not pregnant. She died of stomach cancer soon after. The damage to the young Queen's reputation was huge:

The whole affair has done incredible harm and has played the devil with the Queen's popularity and cast dreadful odium and discredit on the Court... the public takes it up ... on the principle of favouring an injured person.[19]

But whilst Emma, Lady Portman's lack of judgement was soon forgotten and she continued to serve her Queen, her eldest brother's misdemeanours were not.

Lotherton Hall

PLATE 17
The Peris of the North. A portrait of the
Gascoigne sisters c. 1830. Crayon effect
engraving by J. Comson after John Hayter.
PRIVATE COLLECTION

Lotherton Hall

PLATE 18 (ABOVE)
Lotherton Hall, the west front as it
looked in the time of the Gascoigne
sisters (the porch is a later addition).
Photograph, c. 1900.

LEEDS MUSEUMS AND GALLERIES,
LOTHERTON HALL

PLATE 19 (RIGHT)
Parlington Hall. Chromolithograph
by L. Storey, second half of the
19th century.

LEEDS MUSEUMS AND GALLERIES,
LOTHERTON HALL

Lotherton Hall

PLATE 20 (RIGHT)
Castle Oliver, Co. Limerick 1845–50. View from the north-west.

PLATE 21 (BELOW LEFT)
St. Mary's church, Garforth, design for the group of the Virgin and Child in the stained glass of the east window, attributed to Mary Isabella or Elizabeth Gascoigne. Watercolour on paper, c. 1845.

WEST YORKSHIRE ARCHIVE SERVICE, WYL 115

PLATE 22 (BELOW RIGHT)
The Patrick window at Castle Oliver, 1848.

PHOTO: NOEL OLIVER

Nostell Priory

PLATE 23
Portrait of Sir Rowland Winn,
5th Baronet and his wife, Sabine,
standing in the Library at Nostell Priory,
by Hugh Douglas Hamilton, 1767,
oil on canvas.

NATIONAL TRUST

Nostell Priory

PLATE 24

Watercolour sketch entitled 'My Robin, 1814', by Louisa Winn.

PLATE 25

Photograph of Nostell Priory (east front).

Nostell Priory

PLATE 26

The 'Inlaid family cabinet' by Pierre
Gole, shipped to Nostell from
Switzerland in 1781, as part of the
inheritance of Sabine, Lady Winn.

NATIONAL TRUST

Temple Newsam

Temple Newsam

PLATE 29 (RIGHT)
Frances Viscountess Irwin
(née Shepheard), by Benjamin Wilson,
oil on canvas.
HALIFAX COLLECTION

PLATE 30 (BELOW)
The Hon Emily Charlotte Meynell
Ingram (née Wood), by Sir Francis Grant,
oil on canvas.
LEEDS MUSEUMS AND GALLERIES, TEMPLE NEWSAM

Edward, Viscount Lascelles, the eldest son of the second Earl was completely cut off from his family after his marriage to his mistress, whom the family referred to as a 'common prostitute'.[20] This mystery lady was, according to a contemporary account, the sister of Harriette Wilson, the most celebrated courtesan of the age.[21] Unsurprisingly, no portraits of Edward's wife are to be found in the Harewood collection, but she plays her part in the story as it is because of her that Edward was disinherited and the title passed to his younger brother, Henry, who became the third Earl of Harewood in 1841.

Henry, Viscount Lascelles, married Lady Louisa Thynne, daughter of the second Marquess of Bath of Longleat in 1823 (plate 16). Caroline Howard, daughter of the sixth Earl of Carlisle of Castle Howard, had married Henry's brother, William Sebright Lascelles, in the same year, and it is through the letters of Caroline and her sisters that we obtain the best picture of Lady Louisa. Henry and Louisa, Viscount and Viscountess Lascelles, first made their home at Goldsborough Hall, near Knaresborough in Yorkshire, although the family were usually in London between March and September as Henry was an active Member of Parliament. Friends and family turned to Louisa for advice on a whole range of subjects and she was later described as a 'domestic oracle'.[22] Caroline Howard and her sisters, Georgiana Ellis, later Lady Dover, and Harriet Granville, Lady Gower and later second Duchess of Sutherland, were completely in awe of Louisa's calm ability to run the home. Georgiana wrote to Caroline in 1825 to say how much she envied Louisa's 'domestic talents', adding that they were 'what every woman ought to possess'.[23] Over a number of years the three sisters consulted Louisa on many occasions. Caroline, as Louisa's sister-in-law, often visited Goldsborough and whilst there she would seek Louisa's advice, particularly on behalf of Harriet. Louisa was questioned on how to mark household linen and on a particular curtain treatment at Goldsborough and also asked to suggest some 'plans for garden beds'.[24] Georgiana felt unable to raise the salary of her sons' tutor until Louisa had been consulted. Occasionally Harriet was embarrassed to ask what she thought was a 'foolish question', but admitted that she always liked a second opinion; often she would require even more reassurance.[25] In 1832 she wrote to Caroline to recount that her two eldest sons had begun riding lessons. Unsure of herself, she asked, 'Pray tell me at what age Lady Louisa's began to ride, and your husband and his brothers, if their Mama and Papa can remember'.[26] Lady Louisa's responses have not been discovered but presumably she was always happy to help as the requests continued over the years.

Henry and Louisa, by now the third Earl and Countess, moved to Harewood after Henry succeeded his father in 1841 and their family continued to grow. The last of Louisa's thirteen children was born in November 1846 – three months after she had become a grandmother.[27] With this large brood now living at Harewood, plus the extra staff required to service the household, the accommodation at Harewood House was rather cramped. Two years after moving in, the Earl and Countess turned to Sir Charles Barry for help. Barry was at the top of his profession following the success of the new Houses of Parliament, which had been built to his design after the earlier buildings had been destroyed by fire. Louisa would have heard many reports of the architect's work. Her brother, the Reverend Lord John Thynne was Sub-Dean of Westminster Abbey at the time of the fire in 1834 and throughout the period of rebuilding from 1840. Louisa would also have been familiar with the work Barry had carried out for Harriet Granville's family at Trentham, Staffordshire and Lilleshall in Shropshire.

It was for the gardens at Lilleshall that Harriet had sought Louisa's help in planning garden beds. Louisa was clearly a keen gardener and with Barry she planned a new terrace to replace the now dated sweeping swathes of lawn south of the house. Louisa's portrait by George Richmond shows her standing proudly on the new terrace and looking every inch the paragon of domesticity her friends believed her to be. Louisa approved of her 'soft matronly, ladylike appearance' in the portrait, and Henry thought it 'perfect'.[28] Sadly, neither Louisa nor Henry would live to see the portrait hung at Harewood. Henry died in 1857 and Louisa in 1859, and her obituary in the *Leeds Intelligencer* summarised the qualities that made her such a popular and respected lady:

> *The deceased Countess was much beloved by all classes of persons, and her death will be sincerely lamented, as well by the poor as the rich. By her good actions, for the moral, social, and religious advancement of the tenantry on the Harewood estates and other persons, she won well-merited praise, and she descends to the grave with the blessing of many hearts upon her.*[29]

Even with advances in medical science the dangers of childbirth and high rates of infant mortality still caused great grief in many families. All of Louisa's thirteen children lived beyond infancy, although two teenage sons tragically died in March 1845. Louisa's daughter Mary would not be so lucky. Lady Mary Lascelles married the Hon. Sir Robert Henry Meade, a high-ranking civil servant and Groom of the Bedchamber to the Prince of Wales, in 1865 (fig. 5). Mary began a diary on her wedding day and the brief entries record her visits, music and reading as well her time spent creating a fernery. There is no mention of her pregnancy until 20 January 1866 when an entry records the baby's weight.[30] The baby was named Mary, although she was Mia to the family, and the Prince of Wales wrote with his congratulations. But on 7 February Lady Mary died, and the following day the Prince wrote to Sir Robert again:

> *My dear Meade. I have a task before me, perhaps one of the most difficult ones to accomplish... little did I think when I saw you here, so happy, last Tuesday, that in one short day you would have to go through one of the greatest trials that a man can have on this earth... that the Almighty may give you strength to bear this great grief is the prayer of your sincerely attached friend, Albert Edward.*[31]

The last entry in Mary's diary was presumably composed by her husband, as one week after Lady Mary's death it simply states: 'Baby baptised'.[32]

Mary's brother, Henry Thynne Lascelles married Lady Elizabeth Joan de Burgh

FIGURE 5
Lady Mary Meade, by Charles Edward Perugini, c. 1860, oil on canvas.

in 1845. Elizabeth was the daughter of the first Marquess and Marchioness of Clanricarde; her mother was Harriet Canning, daughter of George Canning, Prime Minister in 1825. Elizabeth died in 1854, and so Henry was therefore a widower with six young children when he succeeded his father as Earl in 1857. He remarried in 1858 and his bride was Diana Smyth, daughter of Colonel Smyth of Heath Hall near Wakefield; this union produced a further eight children. The fourth earl and countess seem to have been a frugal couple and there were few changes during their time at Harewood.

Henry Ulick Lascelles, their eldest son, married Lady Florence Bridgeman, daughter of the Earl of Bradford, in 1881, and inherited his father's title and estates the following year. The fifth Earl and Countess preferred a quiet life at Harewood and the Countess enjoyed life out of doors. She enjoyed boating on the lake and had a new boathouse constructed and she brought to Harewood a flock of St Kilda's sheep whose descendants thrive at Harewood today. Florence was also very interested in photography and her views of life at Harewood are preserved in a number of albums. But the quiet life of the fifth Earl and Countess was interrupted in 1922 when King George and Queen Mary announced that their only daughter, HRH Princess Mary, was to marry Henry, Viscount Lascelles (fig. 6). Previously, a British princess would have taken a husband from one of the royal houses of Europe, but anti-German feeling after the First World War allowed Viscount Lascelles to make history. Viscount Lascelles had a distinguished war record and as a result of a bequest from his great-uncle, the last Marquess of Clanricarde, he was also a wealthy man.[33] The Earl and Countess of Harewood were delighted with the news and Florence wrote to her future daughter-in-law:

> I feel perfectly certain that you & Harry are going to live for each other and be the very happiest of people – he does so love his home and with the wife he loves added to it, it will be perfect … You can well imagine the excitement there is here, & indeed in the whole of Yorkshire.[34]

Viscount Lascelles and Princess Mary settled at Goldsborough Hall and a year after the marriage Princess Mary became a mother, giving the King and Queen their first grandson. The son was named George and two years later a second son, Gerald, completed the family.

The fifth Earl died in 1929 and Henry and Princess Mary moved to Harewood as the sixth Earl and Countess. Like Louisa before her, the Princess found a house in need of modernisation. Working with the architect Sir Herbert Baker, Princess Mary created a new suite of comfortable rooms on the state floor. As Princess Royal, the title given to her by the King in 1932, she had a full schedule of official duties at home and abroad, but loved to return to Harewood to hunt and to tend her roses. During much of Second World War Princess Mary shared Harewood House with the British Red Cross who established a convalescent home for officers there. Her husband died in 1947 and the Princess remained at Harewood with her eldest son George, now the seventh Earl of Harewood. She played an important role in opening Harewood to the public in the early 1950s and continued her support of many charities. In 1965 she died suddenly whilst walking by the lake at Harewood with her son and two of her grandsons.

George Lascelles, the seventh Earl, married Marion Stein in 1949 and the couple had three sons; the eldest, David, is the present Viscount Lascelles, a professional film producer who now owns the Harewood Estate and is very much involved with life at Harewood today. The marriage was dissolved in 1967 and George married Patricia Tuckwell, an Australian who shares his love of art and music. The Earl and Countess continue the tradition of patronising contemporary artists and a selection of works is shown at Harewood in Lord Harewood's Sitting Room. A drawing by an Australian artist, Louis Kahan, shows Patricia playing the violin – she was once a professional violinist with the Sydney Symphony Orchestra (fig. 7).

In one sense the women of each generation have fulfilled a very similar role. Each has been expected to be a wife and mother, and to play the traditional female role in the domestic sphere, as well as sharing the myriad official duties expected of a member of the aristocracy. But there have always been women who preferred to flout the conventions, whether they caused scandal by eloping or taking lovers, or, in a lesser way, by daring to intrude into the mainly masculine preserves of science or architecture. These women were prepared to take risks to live the life they wanted. Harewood House, however, is shaped just as much by the women who did not make the headlines. Their contributions to the buildings, gardens and art collections at Harewood must not be underestimated. George, seventh Earl of Harewood, wrote recently that 'houses should change and reflect the lives and tastes of the people who live in them.'[35] The women featured here have been contributing to this process for over 250 years.

FIGURE 7
Patricia Lascelles, 7th Countess of Harewood, by Louis Kahan, 1957, watercolour.

With many thanks to Melissa Gallimore, May Redfern and Terry Suthers of the Harewood House Trust for their help and support.

1   Collection of the Duke of Northumberland, The Duchess of Northumberland's Travel Journal, 1771; British Library, MS 42232, William Tyler's travel diary 1773.

2   'On viewing Mr Lascelles' House at Gawthorp Oct 1770', quoted in Wheater, W., *Some Historic Mansions of Yorkshire* (Leeds, 1888), pp. 104-5.

3   *Leeds Mercury*, 26 September 1775.

4   Nottinghamshire Archives, Foljambe of Osberton Papers, 157/DD/FJ, 1779.

5   National Portrait Gallery, D12984, James Gilray 1782.

6   Lewis, W.S. et al (eds.), *Horace Walpole's Correspondence* (New Haven, 1937-1983, 48 vols.), xxv, 227-8.

7   Garlick, K & K. Cave (eds.), *The Diary of Joseph Farington* (New Haven, 1978-1998, 18 vols), viii, 29-30.

8   Interestingly, the list of stylish gentlemen included the Marquess of Graham, Lady Worsley's lover. *London Chronicle*, 21-23 March 1782, quoted in Foreman, A, *Georgiana Duchess of Devonshire* (London, 1999), p. 85.

9   Jewell, J., *The Tourists Companion, or the History and Antiquities of Harewood* (Leeds, 1819).

10   John Milton's *Il penseroso* and *L'allegro* were amongst his most popular short poems. The heroine of the former is 'devout and pure, sober steadfast and demure' while the heroine of the latter is 'jest and youthful jollity'.

11   Lewin, T.H. (ed.), *The Lewin Letters* (published for private circulation, 1909), p. 10.

12   ibid, p. 83.

13 Harcourt, E.W., *The Harcourt Papers*, Oxford, 1880-1905, 14 vols., vi, 44.

14 Broughton, John Cam Hobhouse (ed. Lady Dorchester), *Recollections of a long life, with additional extracts from his private diaries* (London, 1909-1911, 4 vols.), iv, 20.

15 Rutland, John Henry Manners, Duke of, *Journal of a Tour to the Northern Parts of Great Britain 1796* (London, 1813), p. 260.

16 East Sussex County Record Office, Lewes, Sheffield Papers (not catalogued at the time of consultation).

17 ibid.

18 ibid.

19 Strachey, L & R. Fulford (eds.), *The Greville Memoirs* (London, 1938, 8 vols.), iv, 152.

20 Private collection.

21 The Earl of Lauderdale to Thomas Creevey. Quoted in Maxwell, Rt Hon Sir Herbert (ed.), *The Creevey Papers* (London, 1912), p. 294.

22 Leconfield, Lady Maud (ed.), *Three Howard Sisters* (London, 1955), p. 80.

23 ibid, p. 53.

24 ibid, p. 148.

25 ibid, p. 231.

26 ibid, p. 249.

27 Henry Ulick Lascelles, later fifth Earl of Harewood, was born on 21 August 1846.

28 Royal Academy Archives, London. Richmond Papers, acc. 2002/1, letter from Louisa to Richmond, 1 February 1859.

29 *Leeds Intelligencer*, 12 November 1859.

30 Public Record Office of Northern Ireland (PRONI), Clanwilliam/Meade papers, D/3044/K/2, Prince of Wales to Sir Robert Meade, 8 February 1866.

31 PRONI, Clanwilliam/Meade papers, D/3044/J/1/353.

32 PRONI, Clanwilliam/Meade papers, D/3044/K/2.

33 The second Marquess of Clanricarde was the brother of Lady Elizabeth de Burgh, first wife of the fourth Earl of Harewood. He had no issue and left his substantial fortune to his great-nephew Henry Viscount Lascelles.

34 Princess Mary Archive, Harewood House Trust (not catalogued at the time of writing).

35 Swingler, S., *Lord Harewood at Eighty* (Harewood House Trust, 2003).

Mary Isabella and Elizabeth Gascoigne, parallel lives. Philanthropy, art and leisure in the Victorian era.

ADAM WHITE

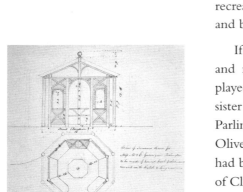

The lives of the Gascoigne sisters illustrate four themes relating to the subject of ladies and the Victorian country house. The first of them is that of sisterhood itself, what it meant and how it affected the patronage in which well-to-do siblings were able to engage. Secondly, philanthropy: where the impulse came from and what its results were. Thirdly, Ireland, a source of revenue to many English landed families, particularly from the seventeenth century onwards: where did the money come from and how was it spent? And fourthly, recreations and pastimes. It is generally assumed that Victorian ladies of good birth and breeding had plenty of leisure. If so, what did they do with it?

If one were to identify a fifth theme, it would be the part played by chance and misfortune in creating opportunities. Accidents of death as well as birth played a major role in the sisters' lives. Mary Isabella was born in 1810 and her sister two years later.[1] They were the daughters of Richard Oliver Gascoigne of Parlington Hall, Aberford, roughly half way between Leeds and York. The Olivers were descended from Robert Oliver, an officer in Cromwell's army who had been granted lands in Co. Limerick.[2] Included in the property was the house of Clonodfoy, which later became known as Castle Oliver, and this Richard was to inherit on the death of his father in 1799, together with a substantial estate. In 1806 he married Mary, the stepdaughter of Sir Thomas Gascoigne, Bt. and through this alliance Richard came into a second estate in England.

The Gascoignes were a very old-established family in Yorkshire where they had settled in the Middle Ages. The line, however, ran out with Sir Thomas. In October 1809, four months before his own death, his only son Tom was killed in a riding accident.[3] Tom's death forced Sir Thomas to remake his will and he designated Richard his heir, on condition that he took the name of Gascoigne and bore the family arms.[4] This was the first opportunity born of tragedy. Richard used it to become, in effect, an Englishman. He seems to have established himself at Parlington before Sir Thomas's death and he remained there, leaving the Irish estates in the charge of his younger brother, Charles Silver.[5] He had four children:

in addition to the sisters there were two brothers, Thomas Oliver and Richard Silver. Events came close to repeating themselves at the end of his own life for in 1842 the brothers both died, followed, within a matter of months, by Richard himself, in April 1843.

Mary Oliver Gascoigne had died in 1815 and the sisters were thus bereaved of all their immediate family. In the process, however, they had become great heiresses with not only the Oliver Irish estates to their names but the Gascoigne Yorkshire estates which Sir Thomas had clearly anticipated would be inherited by their brother Thomas Oliver.[6] It is unclear how well prepared they were for this new role, for very little is known of their upbringing and education. They had grown up in the affluent surroundings of Parlington with its gardens and park (plate 19). There, in 1825 it was proposed to build for them a summerhouse 'to be made of round larch poles, and covered in Thatch & Ling' (fig. 1).[7] That same year Richard Oliver Gascoigne bought the adjoining estate of Lotherton, which included the remains of a medieval village served by an ancient chapel, and a main residence, Lotherton Hall (plate 18).[8] Richard's motive for his purchase can only be surmised, but it is a reasonable inference that he was thinking of his two daughters who were otherwise not provided for. Under the terms of his will the Lotherton estate was placed in trust and assigned to the sisters for life, or until they married.[9] The trust arrangement, which covered the bulk of Richard's property, was also designed to prevent the sisters' share of it from falling into the hands of any future husbands, as would have happened if nothing had been done to prevent it. From all this we may certainly gather that Richard not only cared for his daughters and was mindful of their interests, but that he was also anxious to protect the Oliver Gascoigne inheritance. He may not have been very keen on suitors for his children, for it is noticeable that none of them married in his lifetime. The sisters' looks attracted attention, however; witness a double portrait that was published in print form with a title alluding to their beauty (plate 17).[10] One may imagine that they had no shortage of admirers.

Mary Isabella grew up to be a lady of strong opinions and rare accomplishments. She became intensely interested in the art of turning decorative objects on a lathe, so much so that in 1842, when she was in her early thirties, she produced a book on the subject. *The Handbook of Turning* was published in London and dedicated to the Earl of Craven. It contains 'instructions in Concentric, Elliptic, and Eccentric turning'[11] in a great range of materials, not just wood but also 'gold and silver, brass, iron and copper … ivory … jet, alabaster, and marble … cocoa nut' and even coal.[12] The subject is thoroughly tackled with technical diagrams illustrating the text, which is embellished by numerous turned decorations, presumably the author's own handiwork. In the preface Mary Isabella makes it clear that part of her purpose is to engage women in a pursuit that had previously been a male preserve. 'Why should not our fair countrywomen participate in this amusement?' she asks, '… the taper fingers of the fair sex are far better suited than a man's heavier hand, to produce the requisite lightness and clearness of effect'.[13] In view of this, it is ironic that the author was at pains to

FIGURE 2
Portrait of Mary Isabella Gascoigne used as a frontispiece to her book, *The Handbook of Turning*, 1842.

disguise the fact that she was herself a woman. The book was published anonymously with a portrait frontispiece which is noticeably masculine (fig. 2) and the preface even refers to the writer *himself*. It was still difficult at the time for a female author to command respect and attention; this was, after all, the age of the Brontë sisters who published their novels under male pseudonyms.

Mary Isabella was at pains to point out that turning need not be a purely self-indulgent pastime. One of its uses, she wrote, was for the making of gifts, 'to bestow beautiful and cherished remembrances on absent friends'. She also recommended it as:

> *a most useful auxiliary … to our charitable countrywomen, who employ so much of their time in raising funds for the diffusion of Christianity in far-distant lands, for freeing those wretched captives who linger in the bonds of slavery so abhorrent to the British mind, and for augmenting the comforts of the poor in our own happy land.*[14]

This implies, without the vulgarity of an explicit statement, that turned objects can be made for sale to raise funds for good causes.

A more usual female accomplishment is indicated by the presence of a harp at Parlington in 1843.[15] Two years later, in December 1845, a second harp was ordered for 'Miss Gascoigne' from Erard's London workshops.[16] It is a lady's model, slightly smaller than the man's[17] and was perhaps intended as a replacement for the earlier harp, or in addition to it, so that both sisters could have their own instrument. The harp survives in the collection at Lotherton, together with its original wooden case. It is also likely that the sisters received a well-bred young lady's instruction in drawing and painting. This would have served them well later on.

Their father's death and their subsequent inheritance greatly expanded the sisters' horizons, but it also presented them with considerable responsibilities. All the Irish 'Castles, Baronies, Honors, Manors, Mess[u]ages, Towns, Lands, Tithes and other herediments' which in June 1842 Richard Oliver had bequeathed to his surviving son Richard Silver now came to them, together with his 'Mansion House' at Parlington, 'with the Gardens and Premises thereto belonging and [his] several Fields and other premises usually held therewith'.[18] A major feature of the Parlington estate was the colliery at Garforth in which Richard Oliver Gascoigne had invested a great deal of his time, energy and money. The three pits there were named after his daughters: Isabella, Elizabeth and Sisters; the last of these was sunk in the year of his death.[19] Lotherton was but one corner of the empire and the sisters effectively had no need of it, except to generate income. It was let at the time to a Captain Ramsden and remained a tenanted property.[20]

Because it came to them unexpectedly, the sisters' inheritance was something of a windfall, and they probably felt they had more freedom to use it as they chose than they would have done if they had grown up as the principal heiresses, burdened with parental expectations and sage advice. Mary Isabella's remarks in *The Handbook of Turning* about the activities of her 'charitable countrywomen' have a religious and moral fervour about them, which is characteristic of the period, at

FIGURE 3
'View of the Monumental
Almshouses at Aberford, Yorkshire.
Erected by the Misses Gascoigne
of Parlington 1843-5.' Lithograph
by A. Maclure c. 1845.
LEEDS MUSEUMS AND GALLERIES

least among the female upper classes. This zeal quickly found expression in a programme of charitable works on which the sisters embarked, now that they had the means to do so. In 1843 they opened a school for the miners' children in East Garforth, near the Isabella pit, a sturdy brick building with stone dressings, which still exists.[21] In the same year, a set of almshouses was begun in Aberford.

The Aberford almshouses were the sisters' greatest charitable work. Their purpose, however, was not exclusively charitable for an inscription over the front door, which is repeated inside, explains that they were also erected as a memorial to Mary Isabella and Elizabeth's father and brothers. This explains their highly ostentatious character. They stand proudly on the Great North Road with a large area of greensward at the front, bounded by a thick perimeter wall with a lodge at one end. The architecture is collegiate Perpendicular Gothic, designed to suggest the great charitable foundations of the later Middle Ages. It was designed by George Fowler Jones,[22] a young man then practising in London[23] who was shortly to move to York and who remained there for the rest of his career, becoming a personal friend of the sisters.[24] His aim was to make a major visual statement and in so doing he sacrificed practicality for appearance. In order to give enough length for an impressive façade, he made the building only one room deep which would have made it very difficult to heat and a great deal of space is devoted to large corridors which run down the back.

The charity made provision for only eight people, four men and four women. They were looked after by a matron while a chaplain attended to their spiritual needs, except on Sundays when they were required to attend divine service at the local parish church in Aberford. The almshouses are dominated by a central clock tower, balanced at the south end by a chapel and at the north by a refectory or dining hall, with two groups of four dwellings in between. So as to maintain the proportions of the façade, the inmates' accommodation was arranged on two floors, and this would naturally have created problems when they became too infirm to climb stairs. The charity was endowed with £3,350 of Government consolidated stock which was placed in the hands of four trustees, three of them

FIGURE 4
New Church of St Mary the
Virgin, South Milford, Yorkshire.
Engraving from *The Illustrated
London News*, 5 December 1846.

local clergymen and the fourth a neighbouring gentleman, William Markham of Becca Hall whose estate adjoined that of Parlington on the north side. In order that the value of the endowment should not fall if the price of consols went down, it was stipulated that it should be maintained at the value of 600 bushels of wheat as valued in the market in York each year. The trustees did not own the building, but rented it from the Misses Gascoigne for £200 a year, which was reimbursed to them by a charge on the Lotherton estate.[25] This explains why Mary Isabella and Elizabeth were not on the board of trustees themselves, for as owners of the building they could not be without a conflict of interest.

A print, no doubt commissioned by the sisters, shows the almshouses when newly complete (fig. 3). It is a fascinating depiction of the social scene with the villagers gathered outside the perimeter wall and the inmates inside, while in the background a smart open carriage and pair is seen drawing away from the front door. In the carriage are two ladies, Mary Isabella and Elizabeth, doubtless. The building itself is richly adorned with Oliver-Gascoigne family heraldry and monograms, particularly in the stained glass windows, which light the chapel, entrance hall and refectory. For the communal spaces oak furniture was supplied as monumental as the building itself, and Fowler Jones may well have designed these items too.[26]

While the almshouses were being built, a new parish church at Garforth was also under construction. The rebuilding seems to have been instigated not by the sisters but by the Rector of the church, The Revd George Henry Whitaker. In November 1842/43 George Fowler Jones had submitted to him a proposal for rebuilding the body of the church but retaining the old tower with new buttresses and staircase.[27] This scheme was not proceeded with and on 1 July 1844 a faculty was granted authorising total demolition on the grounds that the old building was 'in a ruinous and decayed state and insufficient for the accommodation of the inhabitants.'[28] While this may have been true – certainly the census records reveal that the population was expanding – the decisive factor seems to be have been the intervention of the sisters who were Ladies of the Manor and defrayed most of the cost of the new building.[29]

The new church – designed, once again, by Fowler Jones – was consecrated on 14 November 1845.[30] Two things, in particular, reveal the sisters' proprietary interest in it. The first is that the tracery of the east window of the old church was removed to Parlington Park and re-erected as a folly, where it still stands. The second is that the new east window, a triple lancet, was presented by the sisters; not only that, but according to an inscription which runs along the bottom of the lights, it was actually made by them. It is difficult to know precisely what to make of this claim. It is hard to imagine that they actually did the leading and the main assembly, but they may have been responsible for the parts that are painted, in particular the group of the Virgin and Child which dominates the central lancet. A large painted sketch for this group, showing it as executed but for a few details, survives among the Gascoigne papers, which are deposited with the West Yorkshire

Archive Service in Leeds (plate 21). This could well be amateur work and seems to show the sisters turning a traditional lady's accomplishment to an unusual, practical purpose.

The sisters also had manorial rights at Sherburn in Elmet, to the east of Lotherton. The manor included the village of South Milford, which had no church of its own and had attracted the attention of the Commissioners for building 'additional churches in populous parishes'.[31] Normally in such circumstances the Commissioners provided the funds, but in this case the sisters obliged and gave an endowment for the church's upkeep, together with a handsome set of communion plate.[32] The building was consecrated on 25 November 1846 and the event was considered significant enough to be reported in *The Illustrated London News* (fig. 4). As usual, Fowler Jones provided the designs and he was sufficiently proud of them to exhibit them at the Royal Academy in London.[33] With the sisters' funds at his disposal, he was able to design a far better building than the Commissioners would have allowed for if had they being paying for it with public money. The style chosen, as at Garforth, is Early English Gothic and for a chapel of ease the structure is quite ambitious with a rose window at the west end, porches to north and west, and an octagonal vestry reminiscent of the chapter house of Westminster Abbey.

The Irish estates inherited by the sisters were far larger than those in Yorkshire, though they were mainly agricultural and yielded less income. In Co. Limerick Mary Isabella and Elizabeth had 19,889 acres and proudly recorded the fact in a magnificent folio volume of maps that was compiled for the purpose in 1845 (fig. 5). The maps show that they owned the entire local town of Kilfinane, the villages of Ballyorgan and Glenosheen, innumerable cottages scattered elsewhere, mills and several larger houses. There was, however, an unfortunate social history attached. The curse of Anglo-Irish land ownership was absentee landlords and Richard Oliver Gascoigne had been one. From the time of Sir Thomas Gascoigne's death in 1810, if not before, he seems to have paid very little attention to his property in Co. Limerick, allowing Castle Oliver to fall into decay and leaving the estate in the hands of his younger brother Charles Silver Oliver. Charles had gained an evil reputation for the brutal way in which he had dealt with insurgents in the area and a collective sigh of relief must have gone up when he died in 1817. Twenty years later the tenants of the Castle Oliver and Darranstown estates had presented Richard with a 'Most Humble address' saying that they would 'rejoice to see a member of Your Honour's family reside at Castle Oliver'.[34] Richard had installed William Oliver, presumably a kinsman, as his agent, living in Charles Silver Oliver's old house, Spa Hill, but this clearly did not fulfil local expectations.[35]

Therefore, there was much to atone for and the sisters seem to have been very conscious of this. In January 1844 it was reported in a local paper that they had recently arrived to stay at Spa Hill on a visit to the Limerick estate. The strength of local feeling is shown by the rejoicing which took place: Kilfinane was illuminated, bonfires were lit on the hills around the town and 'the Kilmallock Temperance and Amateur bands attended for three days; during which there was a

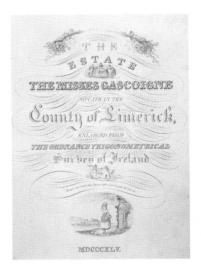

FIGURE 5

'The Estate of the Misses Gascoigne Situate in the County of Limerick.' MS folio compiled by the Hodges and Smith map agency office, Dublin, 1845, title-page.

NATIONAL LIBRARY OF IRELAND, MS. 21 F 122

general order [given] to the shopkeepers to tea, coffee and refreshments to the people.'[36] In the longer term, however, such occasional visits and displays of largesse would not satisfy; what was required was a real, visible and regular presence on the estate. The sisters decided to provide it by rebuilding the castle on a new site, above the old, overlooking Glenosheen to the south. Not only was this a politic way of establishing their visible presence in the area, it also followed the fashion for building houses in positions from which romantic views could be enjoyed, a fashion encouraged by developments in glass technology which made bigger windows possible at reasonable cost. The choice of site would, however, have added considerably to the expense, necessitating as it did the construction of seven great earth terraces for the house and garden. The sisters, however, were not put off. Stories of the fabulous sums they paid still abound in the area. According to one account Elizabeth was shown two sets of designs for the house and chose the more expensive, putting a gold sovereign on the floor and asking the architect if it would build the house to that height.[37] The architect was none other than Mr Fowler Jones who in June 1845 submitted a set of plans that differ only in detail from the building as executed.[38] Tenders for the building of the 'skeleton' were invited through advertisements placed in *The Builder* magazine in July and August.[39] The contract for the stonework was won by Thomas Carroll of Dublin, but for the lighter components, which could more easily be shipped over from England, Fowler Jones turned to his own city of York. John Walker, founder, of that city, supplied ironwork for 'the roof etc.' and his fellow townsmen Henry and John Creaser contracted for the 'internal finishings'.[40]

At this stage the castle was to be known as Glenorthy, a name that the sisters seem to have invented, perhaps to emphasise the fact that they were building anew. It has a more Scottish than an Irish sound, reminiscent of Glenorchy, from which it may have been derived, and it may have seemed appropriate because of the strongly Scottish Baronial flavour of the architecture. It was soon abandoned, however, not seen as tactful perhaps, in view of local sensibilities, and the traditional Irish name of Clonodfoy – variously spelt – was adopted instead.

A more accurate idea of building costs than that provided by local tradition can be gathered from William Oliver's accounts for the Castle Oliver estate. These payments amount to £14,000 between the autumn of 1846 and the spring of 1850, which evidently account for most of the work.[41] Clearly, expense was not spared. The castle is superbly built, mainly in local red sandstone that is used for the whole exterior (plate 20). While the design bristles with historical references, mainly to Scottish architecture outside and Tudor English inside, it incorporates some strikingly up-to-date features. To the west is a massive porte-cochère, masquerading as a castle gatehouse, which allowed the sisters and their guests to drive up to the front door and enter the castle under cover. Mr Walker's ironwork included a very modern system of trusses to support the roofs and the ornamental parts of the balustrade on the terrace that runs round three sides of the house. The building, when complete, was considered interesting enough to be featured prominently in *The Builder*, the leading English journal of architecture and the

FIGURE 6

The Ardpatrick lodge at Castle Oliver, 1848. Engraving from *The Builder*, 23 November 1850.

building trades. The article has two illustrations, one showing the house itself and the other one of the two picturesque lodges which face towards the villages of Ardpatrick and Ballyorgan (fig. 6).

The interior of the castle has − or, regrettably, had − one very special feature. This was noted by *The Builder* as 'the stained glazing of the windows, painted by the Misses Gascoigne'. There were two of them, both very large, in the entrance hall and on the staircase. The top lights of the staircase window, which are the only substantial part of either to survive in situ, are dominated by two monograms of Mary Isabella and there are two corresponding monograms of Elizabeth at the bottom. The rest of the glass was filled with family heraldry and abstract, geometrical patterns, very much like the chapel and refectory windows of the Aberford almshouses.[42] The window of the entrance hall was more ambitious. It was known as the Patrick Window after the series of medallions in the three central lights illustrating the life and works of the Irish patron saint (plate 22).[43] The third piece of glasswork was the chimneypiece in the Large Drawing Room, which had panels worked in *verre eglomisé*, the technique of decorating glass on the back with unfired painting and gilding. *The Builder* noted that these, too, were the work of the sisters. They are also credited by the same source as having painted the panels of one of the doors and the window shutters with Arabesque ornament. There were, in fact, at least twelve doors on the ground floor of the house with painted panels − though it is not clear if they were hand-painted or stencilled − but there is no evidence of painting on any of the shutters.[44]

While Castle Oliver was being built, the Irish potato famine struck. The potato harvest, on which most of the rural population depended for food, was poor in 1845 and in the following year a full-scale disaster developed as the plants withered in the fields and the potatoes blackened and melted away.[45] Unlike some Anglo-Irish landlords, particularly the absentees, the sisters rose to the occasion. They established a soup kitchen to relieve the hunger in Kilfinane and are said to have built walls and roads on their estates to provide work for the destitute. So seriously did they take their responsibilities that they made efforts to provide not only for their own tenants but also for those on the neighbouring estates that were owned by absentees. Corn, flax and carding mills were established at Klifinane to provide extra work and an alternative food supply and it was said that the village was 'for years the asylum of the destitute from all the surrounding parishes'.[46] In order to pay for all this, the sisters are said to have 'spent every penny that they could get, even selling the collections of many years, sometimes, as it would seem, far below their value'.[47] The collections in question are believed to have included 'many race cups and Turf trophies', and a late eighteenth-century race cup, still at Lotherton, commemorating four Gascoigne-owned winners of the St. Leger, is likely to be a case in point.[48]

Castle Oliver was designed for an expanding family. No early plan of the top floor of the house has, unfortunately, survived, but the position and layout of the rooms above the master bedroom suite at the southwest corner strongly suggests

FIGURE 7
Woodlawn, Co. Galway when
newly remodelled in the 1860's.
The group of ladies in the
foreground may include the sisters.
IRISH NATIONAL PHOTOGRAPHIC ARCHIVE,
CLONBROCK COLLECTION

FIGURE 7
Woodlawn, Co. Galway when
newly remodelled in the 1860's.
The group of ladies in the
foreground may include the sisters.
IRISH NATIONAL PHOTOGRAPHIC ARCHIVE,
CLONBROCK COLLECTION

FIGURE 8
The lake at Woodlawn in the
1860's. The couple to the left may
be Lord and Lady Ashtown.
IRISH NATIONAL PHOTOGRAPHIC ARCHIVE,
CLONBROCK COLLECTION

that nursery accommodation was intended.[49] This suggests that the sisters' plans in building the house included their own marriages. Mary Isabella was the first to wed. Her choice fell on an army officer, Captain Frederick Charles Trench of the 66th Regiment who is said to have been stationed in the barracks across the valley at the time.[50] The Trenches were a large and distinguished Anglo-Irish family that could boast two peerages, the Earldom of Clancarty and the Barony of Ashtown, the latter of which had been granted to Frederick's uncle at the Act of Union in 1800.[51] It could thus be argued that his social status was superior to hers but his connections and her money made a near-perfect match and, who knows, it was a romantic era and there could have been love involved. The marriage took place on 15 January 1850. Frederick, like Richard Oliver, assumed the name of Gascoigne in addition to his own and Mary Isabella commemorated the alliance by placing the Trench coat of arms at the top of the Patrick window in Castle Oliver.[52] If there was an element of sisterly rivalry here, Mary Isabella was soon to be upstaged for two years later Elizabeth married Frederick's cousin, Frederick Mason Trench who had succeeded his uncle as the second Lord Ashtown in 1840.[53]

It was not unusual in Ireland for pairs of relations to marry; in fact there was a precedent in the sisters' own family, for their aunts Catherine and Jane Oliver had married two brothers.[54] Under the terms of their marriage settlements the sisters' property was placed in trust and the income divided between the two couples as beneficiaries.[55] Frederick and Mary Isabella settled at Parlington while the Ashtowns took Lotherton, though they appear rarely, if ever, to have lived there.[56] Castle Oliver became their main abode, together with Frederick Mason's own family residence, Woodlawn in County Galway.

It has already been noted that Richard Oliver Gascoigne took pains to protect his daughters' property from whoever they might marry and the legal arrangements revealed in his will[57] would have left them financially in a strong and independent position. Nonetheless, Victorian husbands who married rich ladies had expectations of them and social custom and precedent was very much on their side. It is noticeable that after their marriages the sisters spent less on charitable works and more on projects that were of direct benefit to their spouses. With Castle Oliver now occupied by the Ashtowns, Mary Isabella and Frederick lacked a second home and in 1852-3 they contracted to pay £26,500 for Craignish, an agricultural and sporting estate on the west coast of Scotland.[58] Woodlawn, a plain and unfashionable late Georgian building, was lavishly remodelled in 1855-60 in Sir Charles Barry's Italianate style, employed at such grand English residences as Cliveden and Harewood House.[59] (fig. 7). With its pleasure grounds and ornamental lake fringed by a gravel path, it was now charmingly equipped for gracious living (fig. 8). Churches were built on both estates: that at Craignish was possibly designed by Mary Isabella herself (fig. 9), but the architect's original scheme for Woodlawn was not proceeded with and the building was only erected thirteen years later, on a smaller scale, in 1874.[60]

The sisters may also have deferred to their husbands in the matter of children. Lord Ashtown was a widower when he married Elizabeth, with four children by his first wife, Harriette Cosby who had died in 1845. It was they who became the occupants of the nursery floor at Castle Oliver and Elizabeth had no children of her own. A step-family of four may have been considered enough, besides which Elizabeth was no longer young when she married, particularly by Victorian standards. Mary Isabella, on the other hand, would have been under pressure to produce an heir and it must have been a source of delight and relief that in her early forties she was able to do so quickly, and that the child was male and survived. Frederick Richard Thomas Trench Gascoigne was born in 1851, followed his father into the army and eventually inherited Lotherton on his aunt's death forty-two years later.

To return to the questions with which this essay began, what are we to make of the sisters' relationship? That question has to be answered largely by inference, since none of their personal correspondence, notes or memoranda is known to survive. The first thing that is remarkable about them is how their lives followed exactly parallel courses. They were born within two years of one another, married within two years and died within two years, in 1891 and 1893. In their youth they seem to have done everything together and shared all the same interests, apart from ornamental turning, which, so far as we know, was exclusively Mary Isabella's pursuit. After they married, Mary Isabella continued her artistic activities: *The Handbook of Turning* was reprinted in 1859, and when Aberford parish church was remodelled in 1861-2 she presented the east window which was filled with her own painted glass.[61] There seems to be no evidence that Elizabeth kept up her glass painting, which perhaps suggests that it had been more her sister's passion in the first place. Both sisters, however, remained active in philanthropy: they assisted with emigration schemes from Ireland, which were seen as one solution to the problem of rural over-population, and a whole range of charities is listed in the accounts for Lady Ashtown's portion of the Yorkshire estates in 1881-2.[62] At the end of her life, she moved to Switzerland, but before she went, she set up a charity in Ireland that still exists and dispenses welfare payments in the area around Castle Oliver.[63]

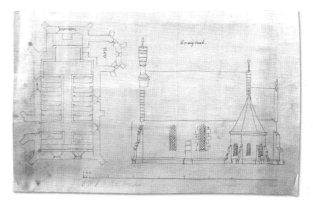

From their marriages the sisters gained status of a kind, but they also lost much: not only did they forfeit their financial independence but even their English manorial rights were taken over by their husbands.[64] It is impossible to resist the conclusion that they knew this would happen and deliberately postponed wedlock until late in the day so that they could enjoy their wealth and allow others to benefit from it. Certainly as mistresses they were greatly beloved. Local tradition in Ireland, which survives in a way that it no longer does in England, supports this for Lady Ashtown, who is still remembered around Castle Oliver, while testimony for Mary Isabella comes for a memorial in Garforth parish church. It was erected, according to the inscription 'as a tribute of respect and esteem by the workmen of Garforth colliery who desire to record their grateful appreciation of the uniform kindness and instructed liberality which has rendered her name beloved by all.' The mineworkers of Garforth had no need to say this and historians are bound to take note of it.

The author wishes particularly to thank four people who have given invaluable help in the preparation of this essay: Mr Nicholas Browne, the current owner of Castle Oliver, The Hon. Roderick Trench, the son of the present Lord Ashtown and the two historians who undertook commissioned research for the *Maids & Mistresses* exhibition at Lotherton Hall (2004), Mr W. J. Connor in Yorkshire and Mr John Kirwan in Dublin.

1   Colman, F. S., 'A History of the Parish of Barwick-in-Elmet, in the County of York, *Thorseby Society Publications*, 17 (1908), p. 160.

2   Oliver, Major-General J. R., *The Olivers of Cloghanodfoy and their Descendants* (3rd ed., London, 1904), unpaginated reprint.

3   See his obituary in *The Gentleman's Magazine*, 79 (1809), p. 990.

4   West Yorkshire Archive Service, Gascoigne Collection WYL 115 (hereafter cited as Gascoigne papers), F2/14

5   Richard is described as being 'of Parlington' in Sir Thomas's will, and a catalogue survives, dated November 1804, of a substantial library which he kept there (Gascoigne papers, additional uncatalogued material, Box 8).

6   This is apparent from his will (cited at n. 4, above).

7   Gascoigne papers, additional uncatalogued material, Box 41.

8   Gascoigne papers, DZ 727 & 728; Ma additional 67; additional abstract of title in additional uncatalogued material, Box 65.

9   A leather-bound copy of the probate copy of this will which belonged to one of the sisters is among the Gascoigne papers; Deed Box 17.

10   The drawing on which this print is based survives in the possession of a descendant of the sisters (private collection, England).

11   *Handbook of Turning* (1842), see title page.

12   *Handbook of Turning*, Preface, pp. xvii-xviii.

13   *Handbook of Turning*, Preface, p. xiii.

14   *Handbook of Turning*, Preface, pp. xiii-xiv.

15   It is mentioned in the inventory compiled on the death of Richard Oliver Gascoigne in 1843; Gilbert, C., *Furniture at Temple Newsam House and Lotherton Hall* (Leeds and London, 1978), vol. 1, p. 234.

16   Gilbert, *Furniture., loc. cit.*

17   Personal communication to the author from Messrs. Munson & Harbour, London who recently restored the harp to playing order.

18   See his will, cited at n. 9, above.

19   Hudson, G. S., *The Aberford Railway and the History of the Garforth Collieries* (Newton Abbot [1971]), pp. 81, 93.

20 Richard Oliver Gascoigne's will names him as the occupant.

21 Hudson, *Aberford Railway*, p. 93. The school was subsequently absorbed into the state system and operated from its original premises until about ten years ago. The building is now a restaurant.

22 His name is on the print (fig. 3) and on an inscription panel in the entrance hall of the building. The same panel names Thomas White as the clerk of works.

23 In 1840 he was at George Street, off Portman Square; Graves, A., *The Royal Academy of Arts. A Complete Dictionary of Contributors and their Work from its Foundation in 1769 to 1904, 4, Harral to Lawranson* (London, 1904), p. 274. By 1844 he had moved to Baker Street; University of York, Borthwick Institute, Fac. 1844/3.

24 He even named his son, who latterly practised with him, Gascoigne Fowler Jones. When the contents of Castle Oliver, the sisters' Irish seat, were sold in 1924, the principal bedroom contained two watercolours of Corsica by Fowler Jones Senior; *Clonodfoy Mansion…Catalogue of Antique and Modern Furniture…* (Kilfinane, Co. Limerick, 1924), p. 34, lot 644.

25 Gascoigne papers, GC Additional 1642 & 1882, Misc 25; *Endowed Charities (Administrative County of the West Riding of York, and the City of Leeds), 4, North Eastern Division, Reports Made to the Charity Commissioners* (London, 1904), pp. 4-6.

26 Gilbert, *Furniture*, pp. 414-5.

27 Yorkshire Archaeological Society, MD 382/11. Unfortunately the paper is cut where the date is written and the last digit cannot clearly be discerned.

28 Pickles, W., *The Parish Church of Garforth*, guidebook (Leeds, n. d.), p. 9.

29 Pickles, *Garforth Church*, p. 11

30 Pickles, *Garforth Church*, p. 10.

31 Two documents of which there are photocopies at the church, attest to this. The first, dated 14 November 1846, releases the freehold of the land, and the copyhold, which was held by the sisters. The second, which is undated, is a petition from the sisters to the Archbishop of York to consecrate the building. The source of the documents is unfortunately not given but they are evidently from the archives of the York archdiocese.

32 Mary Isabella attested to this in a petition opposing the grant of a faculty for alterations to the church in 1878; University of York, Borthwick Institute, FAC 1878/13k, pp. 1-3. According to the *Illustrated London News* report, the sisters were helped by a grant from the Incorporated Church Building Society; I. L. N., 5 December 1846, p. 368. The set of plate consists of a chalice, paten, flagon and alms dish. Each piece is engraved with the names of the sisters as donors and the date 1846.

33 At the 1848 summer exhibition (no. 1179). See Graves, *The Royal Academy of Arts*, iv, p. 274.

34 National Library of Ireland, Ms. 10, 930 part 2.

35 Lewis, S., *A Topographical Dictionary of Ireland* (London, 1837), p. 84; Fleming, J. *Reflections, Historical and Topographical on Ardpatrick, Co. Limerick* (1978), p. 60.

36 *Limerick Chronicle*, 6 January 1844, quoted Fleming, *Reflections*, pp. 60-61.

37 Related to the present author by Mr William Steepe of Glenosheen. See also Browne N., *Castle Oliver and the Oliver Gascoignes*, unpublished typescript (n. d.), p. 27.

38 National Library of Ireland, Ms 4824.

39 *The Builder*, 26 July 1845, p. 360. The advertisement was repeated on 2 August (p. 371) and 9 August (p. 383).

40 'Clonghanodfoy, Co. Limerick', *The Builder*, 23 November 1850, pp. 558-9.

41 Gascoigne papers, additional uncatalogued material, Box 20. This series of accounts, which was submitted half-yearly, goes back to 1843.

42 The windows survived intact until the 1980's when the castle was abandoned and they were largely destroyed by vandals. Parts of the lower lights of the staircase window can be seen in a photograph in the Irish Architectural Archive, Dublin (ref. 4/54 Y3).

43 The Patrick Window is better recorded in photographs than the staircase window (see Irish Architectural Archive 4/54 Y11-12 & 4/54 CS2 6-14).

44 All the painted panels have been removed from the house, although at least one set is known to survive. The appearance of some of the doors in question is recorded, once again, in photographs in the Irish Architectural Archive (4/54 CS4; 4/54 Y 6-8). Further photographs in the Archive record the appearance of the chimneypiece (4/54 Y 9-10).

45 A vivid description of the disaster is given by Trench, W. Steuart, *The Realities of Irish Life* (London, 1869), chapter VII. Trench was a land agent who was a first cousin of the sisters' future husbands, Lord Ashtown and Frederick Charles Trench Gascoigne.

46 Report of The Rev. James Walsh, parish priest and secretary of the Bulgaden Relief Committee in the Barony of Coshlea, Co. Limerick (National Archives of Ireland RLFC 3/2/17/28&31; see also Fleming, *Reflections*, p. 74; Hogg, W. E., *The Millers & The Mills of Ireland of about 1850* (Dublin, 1998), p. 89.

47 Cooke-Trench, T. R. F., *Memoirs of the Trench Family* (privately printed, 1897), p. 112. This somewhat partisan family history, written by a marital relative of the sisters, nonetheless deserves some attention.

48 Lomax, J. *British Silver at Temple Newsam and Lotherton Hall* (Leeds, 1992), pp. 19-20.

49 The bedroom is designated as 'Miss Gascoigne's' on the 1845 plans.

50 This according to local legend, which, however, has him confused with Elizabeth's future husband who was not in the army. See Browne, *Castle Oliver*, p. 4 and Anon., 'Death of Colonel Gascoigne. A Noted Yorkshire Veteran', obituary from an unknown local newspaper, June 1905, archives of the Garforth Historical Society. Frederick's rank and regiment are given in the marriage settlement deeds, cited below at n. 55.

51 Cooke-Trench, *Memoirs, passim*.

52 Browne, *Castle Oliver*, p. 48. The window was originally installed in 1848 and was dated at the bottom (ibid.). The heraldry can clearly be seen in one of the Irish Architectural Archive photographs (4/54 Y11-12).

53 G. E. C., *The Complete Peerage*, s. v. Ashtown.

54 Catherine had married in 1780 the 1st Baron Mount Sandford and Jane in 1789 The Revd William Sandford; *Burke's Irish Family Records* (1976 ed.), p. 922.

55 Public Record Office of Ireland, registry of deeds, nos. 4747-4753. The trust was first established in 1850 and extended when the second marriage took place in 1852.

56 In peerages published during Lord Ashtown's tenure of the title, Lotherton is described as his English seat. The house, though, was let to a series of tenants, including Major The Hon. Frederik Le Poer Trench, Lord Ashtown's son-in-law, who had it in 1883 (see *Maids & Mistresses* exhibition gallery guide for Lotherton Hall, no. 70).

57 See above, note 9.

58 WYL 115/Add box 71 and deed box 17. The documents in the box of additional documentary material include a newspaper cutting dating from June 1852 which advertises the estate for sale. Only £16, 500 was paid until such time as it would be 'cleared of encumbrances'.

59 The architect was, however, not Barry but, almost certainly, a local man, James Kempster of Ballinasloe. A photograph of a watercolour of the house painted in 1853, prior to remodelling, is in the Irish Architectural Archive (C5/422). The dates of the new building are incised on the back of it, at the north and south ends.

60 The date is on the east end of the building. The original designs, by James Kempster, were, until recently kept in the vestry. They were conserved and framed in 2004 for display in the *Maids & Mistresses* exhibition at Lotherton Hall (gallery guide, no. 56).

61 Kirk, G. E., *The Parish Church of Aberford with a Short Notice of Lotherton Chapel, Yorkshire* (Shipley, 1959), p. 15, n. 2.

62 Gascoigne papers, Add 27.

63 Information communicated by Mr Paddy Fenton, a local resident.

64 Frederick Charles Trench became Lord of the Manor of Aberford, Barwick in Elmet and Garforth while Lord Ashtown took the manorial rights at Lotherton and South Milford, see Kelly's *Post Office Directory of Yorkshire* (London, 1857), pp. 63, 89, 223, 541, 657.

Love, rebellion and redemption: three generations of women at Nostell Priory

CHRISTOPHER TODD & SOPHIE RAIKES

This is an account of three generations of women of the Winn family at Nostell Priory, all of whom broke the mould for English upper-class society. Sabine was a foreigner, who married an Englishman for love, against the advice of his family and friends. Esther flouted the rules of the class system and the authority of her mother, by eloping with the family baker. Louisa, the daughter of that baker, was born on a modest small-holding outside Manchester, but returned to Nostell later in life. It is a story of private passion and social alienation, of rebellion and, finally, redemption, hidden within the history of an English country house.

Sabine Winn (1734-1798)

'A passion without thought or reflection': the courtship of Rowland Winn and Sabine d'Hervart

The painting by Hugh Douglas Hamilton of Sir Rowland Winn, fifth Baronet and his wife, Sabine, standing in their library at Nostell Priory, has become an emblem for the eighteenth-century English gentry (plate 23). However, the symbol conveyed is not an entirely true one, as the lady in the picture in fact came from Switzerland. Like his father, the fifth baronet was sent to Switzerland to study as a young man, with his tutor-cum-companion, Isaac Dulon. During his lengthy stay, he became fluent in French and acquired a life-long taste for spending money. He also fell in love with the daughter of a man to whom he had been introduced on his arrival in Vevey on 2 August 1756, Jacques-Philippe d'Hervart.[1]

Born on 25 March 1734, Sabine-Louise d'Hervart was some five years older than Rowland Winn, who was still only seventeen. Moreover, she had been married since 1754, to a much older man, Major Gabriel May, even if she refused to go and live with this serious, hard-working husband. Informed of his son's unsuitable attachment, Rowland's father, the fourth Baronet, swiftly removed him from Vevey to Lausanne in November 1756 (fig. 1). He was assured that 'this little

FIGURE 1

Portrait of Sir Rowland Winn, fourth Baronet, father of young Rowland Winn, by Henry Pickering, 1746, oil on canvas.
NATIONAL TRUST

affair' was now over, and that 'it was only an amusement'.[2] In fact, the affair was far from over and it was soon being said that 'Mr Winn had been giving a little too much free rein to his passion'.[3] When Gabriel May died of cancer in March 1759, in spite of public gossip, young Rowland was soon talking of marriage to Sabine.

Understandably, his father was horrified. Asking Rowland to think again, he dismissed 'this pretended attachment' as 'a passion without thought or reflection', which had only arisen with the death of Gabriel May, and even if by Rowland's account 'she but little cohabitated, there must have been touch on both sides'. He wanted his son to picture a foreign wife at the head of the dinner-table and unable to converse; and reminding him how often he had made fun of French accents, to imagine what it would be like for him even to suspect that anybody was mimicking his wife. He listed the main reasons why he thought Sabine would make an unsuitable bride: above all that love was not enough to ensure a happy marriage 'for without connections and means a man will make but a mean figure in this country'.[4]

Asked to reflect, Rowland dithered. He stopped seeing Sabine for a time, but could not get what his brother called 'that disagreeable affair' out of his mind.[5] His tutor said he could understand Rowland's dilemma all too easily, as Sabine was 'beautiful and amiable', adding, rather less charitably, that he believed that 'her fortune was attracting him a little'.[6] Opposition to the marriage continued among the Winns. In such marriages, according to Rowland's aunt Mary, people 'are lost to the world & never make any figure in life'.[7] Others were more sanguine. Rowland's brother-in-law, Nathaniel Cholmley, wrote to the fourth Baronet that 'as the young woman [had] so good a character and [was] likely to be a good fortune and a protestant', he thought those 'very fortunate circumstances'.[8] Rowland's brother was convinced that he might have found richer pickings elsewhere, but even his aunt believed that a family fortune of £70,000 was not to be sniffed at.[9]

Eventually Rowland's love won the day. He was married to Sabine in Vevey on fourth December 1761 and the couple departed for England the following year.

Life in Yorkshire and London, 1762–1785

In the first years of their marriage – before the birth of their daughter Esther in 1768 and of their son Rowland in 1775 – Rowland and Sabine spent time in London together. They enjoyed the social round, eventually from a town house in St. James's Square (where their children were to be born). Conversation for Sabine was not easy, and when she met people who spoke little or no French, as one mutual acquaintance put it, 'they did nothing but laugh at each other'.[10]

In Yorkshire, the couple first lived at Badsworth, about four miles from Nostell, in a house that had been lent by the fourth Baronet's close friend, the Marquess of Rockingham.[11] There, in March 1763, Sabine experienced the first of the many times she was going to be left alone, while her husband was away. She lived a lethargic existence, in what she called 'one of the more desolate and ill-fated corners of the universe', where the only novelty was provided by his letters:

> *The manner in which I live can better be called vegetating like a plant than like a human being. Besides, I am not in the best of health. I can neither sleep nor eat, which, as you know, are the only pleasures one can indulge in at Badsworth.*[12]

As she said, 'my dear bed holds me to its heart'[13], and she often gives the impression that she was fond of staying there. Obviously, however, she had more to do after the death of the fourth Baronet in 1765, when the young couple moved to Nostell and took over responsibility for the estate (plate 25). Much of Sabine's time was henceforth taken up with hiring and firing staff (both Swiss and English) and settling often violent quarrels between servants. She had to deal with gossipy, quarrelsome housekeepers who spoiled the junior domestic staff and showed no sense of thrift; impudent scullery-maids who refused to milk the cows or make the bread; or servants who even made Nostell seem more like a brothel by having sex in each others' rooms 'twenty times a day'.[14] Finding and keeping cooks seems to have been a particular problem, and she was looking for replacements almost every year right up to the end of her life. One cook, for instance, refused to provide food for her visitors, because they arrived after hours.

Though Sir Rowland was often away in London or on his estates in Lincolnshire, he usually tried to write to her every day. When he was not interviewing new servants and trying to encourage them to come north without their wives, he was, as he said, only too happy to be kept very busy running errands for her, looking for tea and coffee, spermaceti candles, bed linen, silk, calico, perfumed garters – even if they were out of fashion – and oriental slippers (which had to be fetched from France), or having her watches repaired by top London watch-makers such as Thomas Mudge. He also had a small carriage built for her and provided it with a small horse, ordered a bamboo chair for his daughter from Chippendale, and sent up to Nostell a whole menagerie of animals and birds for the children to play with. Sabine copied out advertisements from the newspapers of unusual devices for him to look out for, such as a new water-closet. Above all, she sent him to look at small dogs, which do not always live up to their description. After his death she continued to send people looking for dogs, and even during the French Revolution she had a man scouring France to locate one.

Home-made medicines

As with many people, illness played a large part in the lives of Sabine and Sir Rowland. Sharing her mother's mistrust of British doctors, Sabine showed a particular interest in herbal remedies. Her papers are full of recipes for remedies in French, German, and English for both humans and animals, especial for skin and hair problems (fig. 2). On one recipe for an essence, she commented that it could not be found in London and that she had made it herself.[15] Typical is a remedy against flatulence, written in what would seem to be the hand of the lady's maid who came from Vevey with Sabine.[16] To be taken at bedtime, it consisted of aniseed, fennel, caraway, carrot and coriander seeds steeped in a pint of Spanish

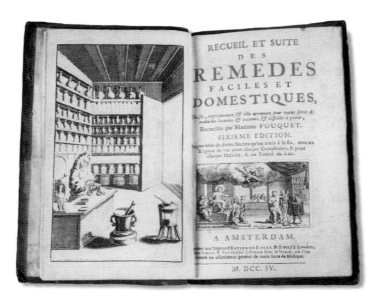

FIGURE 2

Title-page and frontispiece to
Sabine's copy of Marie de Maupeou
Fouquet, *Receuil et Suite des Remedes
Faciles et Domestiques* (1704).

NATIONAL TRUST

brandy for three weeks, to which one then added half a pound of candy sugar dissolved in camomile tea, heated and strained to make a julep. This remedy was considered 'excellent against the upsets and pains of the stomach, as it dissipates undigested matters and winds and strengthens the digestive organs'.

Sabine also copied out articles, such as one for curing dropsy from *The York Chronicle* and adverts for books, including John Mudge's, *A radical and expeditious cure for a recent catarrhous cough* (1779). Following an inquiry from her husband, the bookseller John Murray noted that Lady Winn wished 'to purchase a few books upon officinal botany' and added:

> *Not wishing to spend more time in pursuing the scientific knowledge of vegetables, [Lady Winn] is desirous to be truly informed about the real virtues of simples [or medicinal herbs], and prefers such authors as lay down plain and particular directions how to prepare the best medicines from simples. How they are to be taken and what is a proper dose.*[17]

She noted that she possessed William Salmon's *The New London Dispensatory* (1678) and George Bate's *Pharmacopœia Bateana* (1700), and copied out details from both.

Married Life

The love between husband and wife matured, despite the many separations. Sabine was sharpest with him in her early letters. In 1763 she asked what 'little game' he was up to, refused to beg for him to come home, and signed off by saying that she was now no more than his 'most humble servant', rather than the usual 'his dear Sabine', or rather 'Bibby', who was going to be entirely his for the rest of her life. When he wrote that his return had had to be delayed 'for so many different reasons', she snapped back:

> *For a man who has been able to deceive me and break his word so often, it truly suits him to adopt a harsh tone with his unfortunate wife. Courage, my dear, adopt all the vices of the city in which you have settled down, but be also aware that my mind is made up. I shall set out for London and no longer act tactfully, if you do not come back this week …*[18]

Relations became strained again in October 1775, following the birth of her son. When her husband left her without change to pay her daughter's nursemaid, she broke into English and made a veiled allusion to what sounds like infidelity:

> *I know a certain person who would not be as patient as I am and it is why, I suppose, she deserves to be preferred. <u>This is exactly the state of the case. I could not help, when I began to write, mentioning these circumstances, because I really was very much vexed,</u>*

&c. I hope that you will be delighted with the progress that I have made in the English language.[19]

However, this strain in their relationship seems to have passed and she was soon once more assuring him that she could not love him more tenderly.

Relationships with staff and family

The Winns frustrated some of those whom they employed, but won loyalty and respect from others. Tradesmen complained about unpaid bills, and the Winns were frequently the victims of hearsay. In 1777, the disgruntled husband of one of their daughter's governesses gossiped that the Winns had starved his wife, and that while they doted on their son, they entirely neglected their daughter, who wept from morning till night. However, Sir Rowland often commented that people were still prepared to come and work for them despite the rumours.

It is difficult to know how far to trust the entirely negative representation provided by their cousin, the Unitarian educationalist Mrs Catherine Cappe,[20] since – as she admits – her brother quarrelled with Rowland Winn. In her memoirs she accused the young couple of being thoughtless towards others by keeping late hours. She contrasted Rowland with his father, giving a picture of a vindictive and petty man, jealous of his sister Ann, who had taken over the role of mistress of the house during his absence. As for Sabine, she thought her nature belied her appearance which 'was singularly captivating, for she was very beautiful, and had a great deal of vivacity' with 'fierce dark eyes sparkling with a radiance exclusively their own.' These, according to Mrs Cappe, hid a shallow nature, with Sabine amusing herself at the expense of others behind their backs 'in her broken English'.

Rowland and his wife certainly quarrelled with most of their relatives, and not just on his side of the family where there seems to have been fairly widespread reluctance to accept this foreign wife. He curried favour with his aunt Mary, encouraging her to make him her sole legatee, but otherwise the only members of the family to have remained on affectionate terms were apparently his cousin on his mother's side, Sir Edward Dering (who had spent some time with him in Switzerland), and his sister Charlotte.

Widowhood

After Sir Rowland's sudden death on his way to London at Retford on 20 February 1785, his widow shut herself away at Nostell with her children. Sabine's son, Rowland, a bonny child with a cheerful disposition, had always been the apple of his mother's eye. However, after his father died, he seems to have been largely left to his own devices, especially following the death of his tutor. As a result, the wider family instigated Chancery proceedings to have him educated away from home. Sabine was even threatened with imprisonment. Despite this, Sabine remained fiercely protective of her son, ordering out of Nostell any young lady she suspected of setting her cap at him.

These problems apart, Lady Winn also had to deal with many financial worries caused by her husband's extravagance, and she relied increasingly on the Wakefield solicitor, Shepley Watson, to sort out her affairs. Eventually her health broke down. By 1791, the gout in both her hands was so serious she could not write. She became fat, and by August 1798 she had 'so far lost the use of her limbs as to be obliged to be lifted by two people in and out of bed'[21]. After a short illness, she died at eleven o'clock on the morning of 16 September 1798, with her son not even bothering to inform the other members of his family.

Although Sabine certainly left her mark on Nostell — overseeing for instance an extension to Lower Lake — the initial fears of her father-in-law over his son marrying a foreigner were partly justified. To compound her early difficulties with socialising and the English language, she became ever more reclusive after her husband's death. The family lawyer, Fearfax Fearnley, wrote to her:

> It is a very great pity that your Ladyship who ought to be the companion of kings & princes of the earth, should not even suffer the sun to smile at you, or the wind to blow upon you, but prefer the solitude of the pelican to the pleasure of public life.[22]

Rowland's sharp-tongued sister, Mary Winn, 'knowing too well' her sister-in-law's 'hatred to … all the family', accused her of stopping her son from 'cultivating an acquaintance and friendship with the near relations and friends of [his] late father', and from acquiring 'proper connections in life'.[23]

Sabine's Heirlooms

Sabine was the sole heir of Jacques-Philippe and Jeanne Esther d'Hervart. Upon the death of her mother in 1779, she inherited a fortune of £70,000, as well as her parents' house in Vevey and most of their possessions. The house was eventually sold, but many of its contents, including 'household goods, furniture, pictures, cloathes [sic], and other things late belonging to the said Baroness D'Hervart'[24], were shipped to England in 1781, in seventeen large crates.

Each crate was packed with a bewildering array of different objects. Silver coffee pots and antique gilt bowls jostled with drawing books and horse bridles; blunderbusses and cutlasses with feather beds and books. Eight of the crates were packed entirely with speciality food and drink, including twenty-four Swiss cheeses, 45lb of chocolate, 123 bottles of 'simple Water of Orange Flowers and other plants distilled', and 450 gallons of home-made wine.[25] In a separate cargo, a number of 'beautiful orange trees' were transferred from the Hervart's summer house to Sir Rowland Winn's 'Green House' in the stable block at Nostell.[26]

Of all the Swiss goods imported to England in 1781, only a precious handful survive at Nostell Priory today: eleven 'pictures of ancestors of the family', spread throughout the house; a magnificent 'Inlaid family cabinet', now in the Tapestry Room (plate 26); a collection of books in French and German, hidden away in the upper shelves of the Billiard Room bookcases; and 'parchments, papers and family writings', now stored in a local archive office. Set amongst the famous Chippendale furniture and Old Master paintings, they tell a different story of

Nostell Priory and comprise what must be a unique layer in the collection of an English country house.

Esther Winn (1768-1803)

Childhood

Esther, daughter of Sabine and Sir Rowland, was a bright and spirited child and a tempestuous teenager, whom her parents found difficult to control. Particularly after the birth of her younger brother, Rowland in 1775, she was prone to temper tantrums, probably jealous of her mother's love. Sabine was clearly besotted with her only son, confessing in a letter to her husband, that: 'his company is so precious to me, that it would be easier for me to do without food and drink than to be deprived of the sight of him'.[27]

While he was 'a beautiful and good angel',[28] Esther was characterised as the difficult child (fig. 3). Sir Rowland hardly ever received one of her letters, without finding fault with it. At least one of her governesses complained of her obstinacy. In 1782, she had a blazing row with her father, angering him with 'her air of resistance and her dry and grumpy tone'.[29] As always, she was very contrite after her outburst, making herself sick with worry and writing to her father to beg his forgiveness.

Given her rather stormy home life, Esther's relationship with her absent Swiss grandmother, Jeanne Esther d'Hervart (c. 1710-1779), is particularly touching.[30] Though they never met face to face, they corresponded with each other in French in the late 1770s, when Esther was between seven and ten years old. Jeanne Esther appreciated her granddaughter's 'vitality' and 'passion', praised her 'progress in writing and drawing', and commented upon her fine 'memory and facility for learning'. In return, Esther sent her grandmother 'pretty drawings' of flowers, which the latter framed and hung next to a portrait of the artist in her private sitting room in Vevey.

Though Esther's education was sometimes rather haphazard, she was a bright girl, with a talent for languages and an enthusiasm for reading, drawing and music. In 1790, a friend of the family observed that she wrote a 'beautiful hand', spelt accurately, arranged her ideas with precision, was a 'mistress of French and Italian' and had 'a competent knowledge of music, dancing, &c.'.[31] She particularly enjoyed her drawing lessons, under the tutelage of James Bolton of Halifax, a self-taught botanical artist and naturalist, who introduced her to the flora and fauna of the Nostell park. She was also fond of animals, tending her father's collection of ornamental birds, including a Myna bird and 'male and female Boobies [marine birds] of Siberia', with her French governess, Madame Le Picq.[32]

Elopement

Sir Rowland's sudden death in 1785, was a devastating blow for Esther. Sabine shut herself away at Nostell Priory, spurning the company of family and friends and

FIGURE 3
Portrait of Esther Winn, English School, before 1792, oil on canvas.
WEST YORKSHIRE ARCHIVE SERVICE,
BY KIND PERMISSION OF LORD ST. OSWALD

taking solace mostly in her beloved son. She refused an invitation from her sister-in-law, Charlotte, for her daughter to spend some time in London, adding mysteriously that she was 'unwilling to have her beyond the reach of [her] eye and inspection, for reasons [she could not] mention by letter'.[33] Thus, at the age of seventeen, Esther found her world contracting, just when it should have been opening out.

According to her own later account, Esther spent the next seven years 'faithfully attend[ing]'[34] upon her mother, with only her younger brother and the domestic staff for company. However, she could not stay closeted at Nostell forever. At the beginning of the 1790s, the family lawyer said that he had 'heard it repeated in company that Miss Winn was about to elope with the apprentice of a glazier & that post horses paraded before the gates at Nostell night after night to convey her away'.[35] Finally, in 1792, she ran away to Manchester with John Williamson, the handsome Nostell baker, whom she married by special license in 1793.

Following her elopement, Esther was paid an annual stipend of £450 from the Nostell estate, as the interest upon the sum of £10,000, left to her by her Swiss grandmother. Otherwise, Sabine completely disowned her daughter, cutting her out of her will and even refusing to see her when she herself was dying. As Esther noted, despite her own desire for reconciliation, her 'mother at the trying hour still held [her] in the same contempt'.[36]

Married life in Manchester and Lincolnshire

John and Esther Williamson settled in rented property, first at 4 Dickinson Street, near St Peter's Church in Manchester, where their sons John and Charles were born in 1794 and 1795. They later moved to Longsite, near Manchester, where their daughter, Louisa was born in 1798, and finally to a smallholding in Morton, near Gainsborough in Lincolnshire, close to John's family. This last house had six rooms, a courtyard with a brewhouse and dairy and a small plot of land, enough for a haystack, two cows, two calves and two pigs.[37]

Esther adapted to her new circumstances with a good grace. Her aunt, Mary Winn, with whom she maintained contact, was pleased to hear how well she 'conducted [herself] and is respected by all [her] acquaintance'.[38] She employed a young girl as a maid of all work, but had to learn the practical skills of housekeeping. In the early years of their marriage, she asked her husband's advice upon such matters as the storage of butter and the hiring of a new maid, and reported to him, with some pride, that 'I am very busy, just going out to market for meat. I get it twice a [week? as] it will not keep'.[39] With John's encouragement, she also struggled to maintain her former interests; amongst the few items she requested from Nostell Priory, were her drawing books and pianoforte. Though her appeals were ignored by her angry mother, she managed to acquire a cheaper piano, which dominated the 'Best low front room' of their house in Morton. John was very proud of his wife's accomplishments, writing to her from his parents' house in Scotter in Lincolnshire in 1795:

My dear love, I am very glad that you get so far forward with your music as I shall take very great delight in seeing your little fingers go. It will please me very much and I shall expect you to play me a good many tunes when I come back.[40]

John and Esther seem to have been a truly devoted couple and it appears that she found happiness in her married life. However, it was relatively short-lived as John, who was often unwell, died from a protracted consumptive illness in 1799. Esther was heart-broken at her loss and wrote to her friend, Mrs Lockwood that 'I seem fallen from a great height & stunned [so] as to have scarce any sense or feeling'.[41] Another friend, realising her vulnerable state, warned her that 'Your fortune will now be the greatest object for men to hunt after. On that account you will have many offers, but mind what I say. It will not be by those who have 500 per year'.[42] Perhaps afraid of her lonely position, she rushed headlong into a second marriage in 1801, surprisingly with another man called John Williamson. This was not a happy union and they were separated the following year. Esther herself died in 1803, at the age of thirty-five, and was buried in Morton, next to her first husband. She left three orphaned children, John, aged nine, Charles, eight and Louisa, five.

Louisa Williamson, later Louisa Winn (1798-1861)

Louisa Williamson was born in 1798, just a year before her father died (fig. 4). She lived with her mother, Esther, and her elder brothers, at Morton in Lincolnshire, about eight miles from her paternal grandmother and other Williamson relations in Scotter. When her mother died in 1803, this little world was broken apart. Esther had never been reconciled with her family at Nostell Priory. However, her younger brother, Sir Rowland, sixth Baronet was still unmarried, which meant that her eldest son, John was the rightful heir to the Nostell estate. In a sudden reversal of fortune, all three of Esther's children were taken into the guardianship of the sixth Baronet. However, they did not live with him at Nostell: John was sent to the Revd Wilkinson's school near Halifax and Charles, who had a damaged foot, to a tutor, close to doctors in London. Likewise, five-year-old Louisa was separated from her family and put into the care of the 'Misses Hemingway' in Sandal, a few miles south of Wakefield.

While her brothers passed through preparatory school, to Eton and eventually Cambridge, Louisa moved from Sandal to her great Aunt Strickland's House at Hildenley in East Yorkshire, where she lodged with her governess, Miss Elizabeth Hill. When Aunt Strickland died in 1813, she and Miss Hill moved to Bath, where the latter set up a small school for young ladies in Widcombe Crescent. This was Louisa's home for the next seven years, until she was twenty-one. She was carefully separated from her lowly Williamson relations, whom the Winn family lawyer visited in 1806, 'to fix their minds not to interfere at Nostell'.[43] However, she continued to correspond with them, until her brother, John, persuaded her to give up the connection in 1813. Upon their coming of age, all three children changed their name from Williamson to Winn.

FIGURE 4

Cut-out silhouette of a girl at a writing table by Louisa Winn, c. 1815.

Louisa met up with her brothers at irregular intervals, initially in the school holidays, but then much less often, as the boys started to travel in England and on the Continent. However, they maintained a regular and affectionate correspondence.[44] John adopted a fatherly attitude to his little sister, enquiring after her lessons, and sending her pocket money in the post. He was particularly solicitous about her collection of 'beasts and birds', comprising squirrels, a robin and other small birds, which she referred to as her 'family' and carried with her from home to home. In 1814, he teased her that she was 'becoming a formidable rival to Mr Polito of Exeter Change', the owner of a famous nineteenth-century travelling zoo (plate 24).

FIGURE 5
Early nineteenth-century watercolour painting by James Hewlett, who served as Louisa Winn's drawing master.
NATIONAL TRUST

At Miss Hill's school in Bath, Louisa learnt to speak French and Italian, draw flowers and landscapes, play the harp and piano, and dance and sing. Like her mother, she was very fond of drawing, receiving tuition from the professional flower painter, Mr Hewlett of Bath, who later courted and married Miss Hill (fig. 5). She also had a flair for languages, and, as she explained to John, had 'pretty good practice in [them] as we are always obliged to speak [French] till seven in the evening …'. Louisa and her friends occasionally went to concerts in Bath, but, as John admitted, 'M[iss] Hill's system does not allow of your entering much into the amusement of the place'. She gained many of her pleasures vicariously, by following her brothers' adventures, and always awaited their letters with great eagerness.

Louisa's correspondence with John and Charles in 1816-17, whilst they were on the Grand Tour in Europe, is particularly poignant, as she would clearly have loved to have been there with them. She encouraged them to employ 'a master for the Italian language whilst you are in Italy as you really ought to be able to speak it', and asked them to promise to take her with them 'a year or two hence to make another tour'. She commissioned John to acquire a variety of presents, including 'real Roman harp strings', 'artificial flowers' from Genoa, which Mr Hewlet had recommended as 'very good studies for painting when natural flowers cannot be procured', and a number of Italian books, including works by Petrarch and Ariosto. She also encouraged Charles in his collecting interests, reminding him to bring back 'curiosities from Herculaneum' and 'a collection of lavas and marbles to make two tables for Nostell'. Louisa had already formed her own collection of geological

FIGURE 6
Pastel portrait of Charles Winn, c. 1850, brother of Louisa, who inherited Nostell Priory in 1817.
BY KIND PERMISSION OF LORD ST. OSWALD

specimens, starting with 'a piece of stone from Ireland', which John had picked up for her in 1814.

John inherited Nostell Priory upon the death of his uncle, the sixth Baronet in 1806, though the house was shut up until he came of age. However, he died tragically from an unspecified illness whilst travelling in Naples in 1817. Thus, Charles became the new owner of the family estates and moved into Nostell with his young wife, Priscilla, in about 1819 (fig. 6). Louisa, who never married, lived partly with her brother and sister-in-law, and partly with friends and relations across the country. She continued to share Charles' passion for collecting, accompanying him to salerooms, cataloguing his paintings and assisting him in his project to fill the windows in Wragby Church with ancient stained glass. She died in 1861.

Conclusion

Neither Sabine nor Esther conformed to the conventions of English country house society. Sabine paid for her foreignness with social isolation and Esther for her elopement and marrying so far beneath her station, with rejection by her closest family. However, Louisa, by submitting herself to the will of family and friends, was forgiven her lowly birth and accepted back into Yorkshire society. Her brothers inherited Nostell Priory, where she lived for much of her adult life in comfort and contentment. They show how the lives of the women of the country house could be as complicated and difficult for elites as it was for the rest of British society, both then and now.

1 Our main sources of information are the Nostell Priory Papers, held by the West Yorkshire Archive Service (henceforth WYAS) in Leeds and the registers of the reformed church in Vevey kept in the Archives Cantonales in Lausanne. A more detailed study of Sabine Winn and of her husband is due to appear in the *Yorkshire Archeological Journal*. Our thanks go to its editors for permission to reproduce part of the material here.

2 WYAS, NP/A1/4/15, Letter from Mr Dulon to the fourth Baronet, October 1756.

3 WYAS, NP/A1/4/15, Letter from Mr Dulon to the fourth Baronet, August 1757.

4 WYAS, NP/A1/1509/7, Letter from fourth Baronet to his son, Rowland, June 1759.

5 WYAS, NP/A5/1541/14, Letter from Edward Winn to his father, the fourth Baronet, 30 November 1760.

6 WYAS, NP/A1/4/15, Letter from Mr Dulon to the fourth Baronet, July 1759.

7 WYAS, NP/A4/1509/39, Letter from Mary Winn to her brother, 7 June 1760, quoting the case of the tenth Earl of Pembroke, who had married a foreign lady who had 'all the accomplishments possible'.

8 WYAS, A4/1509/8, Letter of 24 April 1760. Nathaniel Cholmley of Howsham, Justice of the Peace and M.P. for Aldborough and Boroughbridge, married Catherine Winn on 13 June 1750 (*The Newcastle Courant*, 23 June 1750).

9 WYAS, NP/A5/1541/14 & NP/A1.1541/22, Letters from Edward and Mary Winn to the fourth Baronet, 30 November 1760 and 5 April 1760.

10 WYAS, NP/A4/1541/5, Letter from Lady Charlotte Erskin to her father, 19 August 1762.

11 *Memoirs of the life of the late Mrs. Catharine Cappe, written by herself* (London, 1823), p. 97.

12 WYAS, NP/A4/1535/15, Letter from Sabine Winn, Badsworth to Rowland Winn, early 1760s.

13 WYAS, NP/A1/5/8, Letter from Sabine, Lady Winn to the fifth Baronet, 30 July 1776.

14 WYAS, NP/A4/1530/69, Letter from Sabine, Lady Winn to the fifth Baronet, 5 September 1769.

15 WYAS, NP/A4/1538/17, Note, n.d.

16 WYAS, NP/A4/1558/83, Recipe, n.d.

17 WYAS, NP/A4/1538/17.

18 WYAS, NP/A4/1558/166, Letter from Sabine Winn to Rowland Winn, 3 April 1763.

19 WYAS, NP/A1/4/16, Letter from Sabine, Lady Winn to the fifth Baronet, October 1775. The passage underlined was written in English in the text. She had made significant progress in the language since first coming to England, when her father-in-law commented that though she soon understood what was said, she made slow progress in learning to speak English herself, and added the wry comment: 'nor can I say that she takes any delight in learning of it'.

20 *Memoirs of the life of the late Mrs. Catharine Cappe*, pp. 78-103.

21 WYAS, NP/A4/1542/7, Letter from Mary Winn to her niece, Esther Williamson, 1798.

22 WYAS, NP/A4/1594/29.

23 WYAS, NP/A4/1542/7, Letters from Mary Winn to her niece, Esther Williamson, 3 December 1798 & her nephew, Rowland Winn, 9 May 1791; NP/A4/1542/6 and NP/A1/13.

24 WYAS, NP/A1/5/16, Petition by the fifth Baronet to 'Right Honourable the Lords of His Majesty's Treasury', 1781.

25 WYAS, NP/C4/1/8, Inventory of the Furniture and effects brought to England by the fifth Baronet from the estate of his father-in-law, Baron d'Hervart, n. d.

26 WYAS, NP/A4/1558/178, Letter from P. Emanuel Couvreu, Vevey, to the fifth Baronet, Nostell, March 1784.

27 WYAS, NP/A4/1535/2, Letter from Sabine, Lady Winn, Nostell to the fifth Baronet, 26 October 1775.

28 ibid.

29 WYAS, NP/A1/5A/8, Letter from Madame Le Resche to Sabine, Lady Winn, 1782.

30 WYAS, NP/A1/5A/1.

31 WYAS, NP/A4/1538, Letter from Charles Mellish to Mr Maddocks, 1790.

32 WYAS, NP/A4/1535/13 and NP/A1/5A/3/59, Letters from Sabine, Lady Winn to the fifth Baronet, 5 July 1776 and from the fifth Baronet to Sabine, May 1774.

33 WYAS, NP/A1/5A/10, Letter from Sabine, Lady Winn to Charlotte Winn, 25 May 1785.

34 WYAS, NP/A4/1556/2, Letter from Esther Williamson to Shepley Watson, c. 1799.

35 WYAS, A4/1539/6, Letter from Fairfax Fearnely, Halifax, to Shepley Watson, Wakefield, undated.

36 WYAS, NP/A1/6A/4/2, Letter from Esther Williamson to Shepley Watson, 11 December 1799.

37 WYAS, NP/A4/1556/16, An Inventory of the Goods and Chattles of the late John Williamson, c. 1799.

38 WYAS, NP/A4/1542/14, Letter from Mary Winn to Esther (called Sabina) Williamson, 3 May 1797.

39 WYAS, NP/A4/1542/20, Letter from Esther Williamson to John Williamson, 3 August (n.d.).

40 WYAS, NP/A4/1556/9, Letter from John Williamson to Esther Williamson, 23 July 1794.

41 WYAS, NP/A4/1556/5, Letter from Esther Williamson to a friend (Mrs Lallemand?), June (n.d., c. 1800).

42 WYAS, NP/A4/1556/7, Letter from Mrs Gould to Esther Williamson, 8 December 1800.

43 WYAS, NP/A1/7/3, Shepley Watson's account book, 10 April 1806, p. 7, NP/A1/7/3.

44 WYAS, NP/A1/9/1-2, Correspondence of John Williamson and Louisa Williamson, 1808-1816.

Temple Newsam: a Woman's Domain

JAMES LOMAX

The exhibition *Maids & Mistresses* shown at Temple Newsam in 2004 offered an opportunity to focus attention on an important aspect of the history of the house and those who lived and worked in it. The great Tudor-Jacobean mansion (plate 27) lying just four miles from the centre of Leeds in its 1,200 acre park has been in public ownership since 1922 when it was sold for a nominal sum by Lord Halifax. Its entire collections were dispersed and the house slowly developed as a fine and decorative art museum while its story as a five-hundred-year-old house and home was given little prominence. Over the past few years however, great numbers of original artefacts have been repatriated, considerable research undertaken, and a huge programme of restoration almost completed. The exhibition therefore allowed a celebration of the renaissance of Temple Newsam as a great historic house.

In order to keep the subject within bounds it has been decided to concentrate on three principal characters and their households: Isabella, wife of Arthur third Viscount Irwin (c.1670-1764), Frances, wife of Charles ninth and last Viscount Irwin (1734-1807), and Emily Charlotte, wife of Hugo Francis Meynell Ingram (1840-1904). This study will begin by briefly considering their private lives and then move on to compare their different approaches to their responsibilities in the household and in the wider world.

Three Ingram women: Isabella, Frances and Emily

Isabella Irwin (née Machell) (c.1670-1764) (plate 28) was the daughter and heiress of John Machell of Hills, Sussex. Her fortune included the fine Elizabethan house as well as the pocket borough of Horsham that returned two MPs to parliament. She married Arthur, the future third Viscount Irwin in 1685. After her husband died in 1702 she continued to live at Temple Newsam supervising the education of her nine children, all sons (family tree 1). On the marriage of her second son Rich, fifth Viscount Irwin, to Anne Howard, Isabella moved to Windsor where she lived until her death aged ninety-four in 1764, having outlived all her own

I propose … to set out for my own real home at Temple Newsam & there to remain

Frances Viscountess Irwin to Susan Countess Gower, 8 August 1779.[1]

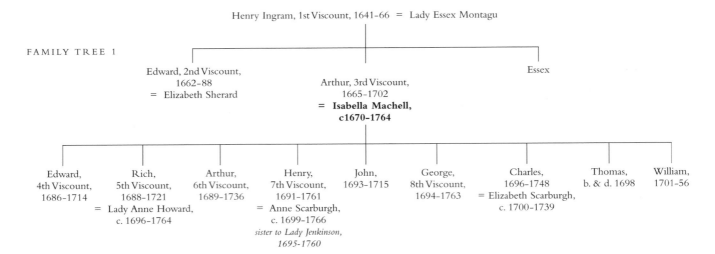

FAMILY TREE 1

Henry Ingram, 1st Viscount, 1641–66 = Lady Essex Montagu

Edward, 2nd Viscount, 1662–88 = Elizabeth Sherard

Arthur, 3rd Viscount, 1665–1702 = **Isabella Machell, c1670–1764**

Essex

Edward, 4th Viscount, 1686–1714

Rich, 5th Viscount, 1688–1721 = Lady Anne Howard, c. 1696–1764

Arthur, 6th Viscount, 1689–1736

Henry, 7th Viscount, 1691–1761 = Anne Scarburgh, c. 1699–1766 *sister to Lady Jenkinson, 1695–1760*

John, 1693–1715

George, 8th Viscount, 1694–1763

Charles, 1696–1748 = Elizabeth Scarburgh, c. 1700–1739

Thomas, b. & d. 1698

William, 1701–56

children. Here she lived in considerable independent style on her jointure of £1,050 a year, frequently visited by her sons, grandson and two granddaughters.

In contrast to her husband, whom she adored, Isabella was highly intelligent, well read, and a keen collector of works of art and fine furniture.[2] Her letters reveal a lively and enquiring mind, full of wit and humour.[3] She was kind to her servants and on good terms with them. Her sons held her in considerable awe and she could be extremely ill tempered if crossed.

Isabella did much to mend the financial losses following the disaster of the South Sea Bubble of 1720 when Rich bought £10,000 of stock for £40,000, mainly on borrowed money, and then died intestate. She was a trustee and executor of the estates of her husband and three of her sons and was assiduous in protecting the family's interests. For example she contributed £1,000 from her own pocket to finally secure the family's political supremacy at Horsham.[4] Likewise she threatened litigation against her elder sons in order to protect the interests of the younger ones.[5]

Frances Viscountess Irwin (1734–1807) (plate 29) was the illegitimate daughter and heiress of Samuel Shepheard, a highly successful businessman and politician, who had refused to marry the girl's mother. Frances' potential fortune of nearly £60,000 made her a considerable catch on the marriage market. Nevertheless she was determined to marry the relatively impoverished Charles Ingram, future ninth

FAMILY TREE 2

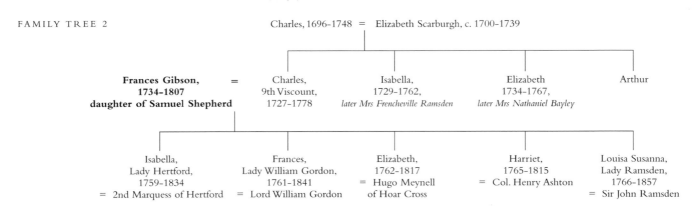

Charles, 1696–1748 = Elizabeth Scarburgh, c. 1700–1739

Frances Gibson, 1734–1807 daughter of Samuel Shepherd = Charles, 9th Viscount, 1727–1778

Isabella, 1729–1762, *later Mrs Frencheville Ramsden*

Elizabeth, 1734–1767, *later Mrs Nathaniel Bayley*

Arthur

Isabella, Lady Hertford, 1759–1834 = 2nd Marquess of Hertford

Frances, Lady William Gordon, 1761–1841 = Lord William Gordon

Elizabeth, 1762–1817 = Hugo Meynell of Hoar Cross

Harriet, 1765–1815 = Col. Henry Ashton

Louisa Susanna, Lady Ramsden, 1766–1857 = Sir John Ramsden

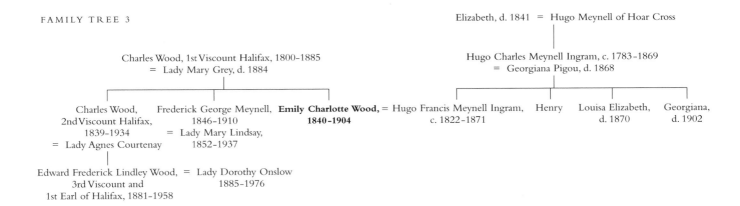

FAMILY TREE 3

Elizabeth, d. 1841 = Hugo Meynell of Hoar Cross

Charles Wood, 1st Viscount Halifax, 1800–1885
= Lady Mary Grey, d. 1884

Hugo Charles Meynell Ingram, c. 1783–1869
= Georgiana Pigou, d. 1868

Charles Wood,
2nd Viscount Halifax,
1839–1934
= Lady Agnes Courtenay

Frederick George Meynell,
1846–1910
= Lady Mary Lindsay,
1852–1937

Emily Charlotte Wood,
1840–1904

= Hugo Francis Meynell Ingram,
c. 1822–1871

Henry

Louisa Elizabeth,
d. 1870

Georgiana,
d. 1902

Edward Frederick Lindley Wood,
3rd Viscount and
1st Earl of Halifax, 1881–1958

= Lady Dorothy Onslow
1885–1976

and last Viscount Irwin of Temple Newsam. After at least two years of negotiations between her trustees and the Ingram family (which required a private Act of Parliament),[6] they were finally married in 1758.[7]

Frances was deeply smitten by Temple Newsam where she spent as much time as possible, giving every excuse to avoid going to London.[8] Almost immediately, great improvements were put in hand in the house and park, and these continued throughout her long life. They included the re-landscaping of the park by Lancelot 'Capability' Brown, the re-building of the south wing, frequent re-furnishing and decorating campaigns,[9] as well as purchases of paintings and works of art.[10]

To their great delight she and Charles produced five daughters who were brought up in a sheltered and civilised ambience before finding husbands and being successfully launched into the world (family tree 2). By this time Frances was a widow and found a new interest in managing the family's pocket borough of Horsham, with its two parliamentary seats, for the Tory cause.[11] A woman of great style, wit and charisma, she died in 1807, as her epitaph says, genuinely 'lamented by all that knew her'.

Emily Charlotte Meynell Ingram (1840-1904) (plate 30) was the daughter of Charles, first Viscount Halifax and Mary, daughter of Charles second Earl Grey. She was a precocious child but highly gifted intellectually and artistically.[12] In 1864 she married Hugo Francis Meynell Ingram, the last surviving descendant of Sir Arthur Ingram who had rebuilt Temple Newsam in 1622. The Meynells main seat was at Hoar Cross in Staffordshire, but they used Temple Newsam for shooting parties in the autumn. He was eighteen years her senior but even so their marriage was very happy, despite political differences between the two families. Emily was unable to have children, possibly because of a riding accident, and so when her husband died in 1871 she inherited all the Meynell Ingram properties.[13] In her distress, and mindful of her great inheritance, she came to rely on her own family, the Woods; her younger brother Frederick, his wife Lady Mary, and their family all came to live at Temple Newsam (family tree 3).[14]

Emily took great consolation in her Anglo-Catholic faith, spending much time and money in building churches and endowing charitable institutions.[15] She had a good eye for works of art that she collected enthusiastically, and was passionately fond of yachting on her beloved *Ariadne*.[16] (fig. 1) She and her husband had just rebuilt Hoar Cross before he died, and she spent much time there, creating its celebrated gardens, and in London, maintaining a full establishment in each place.

As she grew older Emily became increasingly fond of Temple Newsam. She deliberately enhanced its special atmosphere and historic character with the new chapel,[17] the Oak Staircase,[18] the Darnley Room and Dining Room.[19] Although often considered by outsiders to be a diffident person, this could have been explained by her natural shyness, which was compounded by the disappointments and anxieties arising from circumstances. Nevertheless her family and servants were devoted to her.

Love and Marriage

How charming is a husband who tastes and enjoys these apparent trifles & who can live happy & always Chearful [sic] for weeks tête-à-tête with his wife.
Frances Ingram (later Viscountess Irwin) to Lady Susan Stewart, 1759.

The three principal characters of this study, Isabella, Frances and Emily, all enjoyed very happy marriages. Theirs were far from the loveless contracts sometimes arranged between great families. Indeed, in each case the wife had something of a struggle to marry the husband of her choice. Isabella's family were discouraged by her future husband Arthur's disreputable pre-marital behaviour;[20] Frances' trustees thought the Ingrams were only after her money;[21] and Emily's family were Whigs while her husband's were Tories. Thus their paths to the altar were by no means straightforward. Even after their marriages some prejudice lingered which, in Emily's case, lasted into widowhood.[22]

The only member of the Ingram family who seems to have made a serious error of judgement in her choice of husband was Frances' second daughter and namesake ('the wildest of my daughters'), who married the notorious rogue Lord William Gordon in 1781. It seems that her persistence (and his charm) won over her mother and even the Lord Chancellor who had to give his approval, as she was a minor.[23] Although they had a romantic retreat in the Lake District, and she remained devoted to him, Lord William became an infrequent visitor to Temple Newsam. Showing her characteristic generosity, Frances semi-adopted one of his illegitimate sons, bequeathing him a small estate in Lincolnshire at her death in 1841.[24]

The deep affection in which the young people held each other is evident throughout their correspondence in which they use their private nicknames: 'Penny' for Isabella, 'Kitten' for Emily.[25] Each of them grieved devoutly when they were widowed; at first Emily felt bitter and cheated but eventually her faith saved her from prolonged introspection. Her return to Temple Newsam after her husband's death evidently traumatised her.[26] One hundred and fifty years earlier Lady Anne Howard's grief at the unexpected death of her husband, Rich, fifth

FIGURE 1
The *Ariadne* c. 1890.
LEEDS MUSEUMS AND GALLERIES,
TEMPLE NEWSAM HOUSE

Viscount, had caused great alarm to her family.[27] This was also an occasion when the affairs of the heart were allowed to override those of the law. On becoming a widow in 1721 Lady Anne removed a number of items from Temple Newsam that she felt she was entitled to, which she was later obliged to return. This included a portrait of her late husband which however she refused to relinquish 'upon any consideration whatever'.[28] In the end she returned it when she re-married in 1737.[29]

Marriage Settlements and Jointures

The women who married into the Ingram family did so as a matter of personal choice, but the fate of their property was a matter of wide concern and was covered by the legal provisions of their marriage contracts. Until the Married Women's Property Act of 1882 the property of married women was deemed to pass to their husbands on marriage, and only spinsters and widows could own property independently. Thus in order to provide for a daughter's possible widowhood, a father would convey a capital sum, her 'marriage portion', to her husband's family in exchange for a guaranteed pension for her or a 'jointure'. The sums involved could be quite large, and in the unlikely event of there being several widows alive simultaneously (as there were at Temple Newsam) the drain on the estate revenues could be devastating. Thus in 1717 Lady Anne Howard's father the third Earl of Carlisle provided Rich, fifth Viscount Irwin with £8,000 (£6,000 immediately and £2,000 on his death) in exchange for a jointure of £800 p.a., which she continued to draw for the forty-three years of her widowhood. The jointure of Isabella, widow of the third Viscount (which ran for sixty-two years), was £1,050 p.a., and that of Anne, widow of the seventh (five years), was £1,000 p.a. Thus by the early 1760s there were three widowed Viscountess Irwins drawing nearly £3,000 a year on a heavily mortgaged estate whose income barely amounted to this sum. Their deaths in quick succession enabled Charles, ninth Viscount to invest in his estates with greater confidence.

Because of her great wealth and the difficult provisions of her father's will, the marriage contract of Frances and Charles, ninth Viscount, was extremely complex and required a private Act of Parliament to effect.[30] In exchange for her fortune of nearly £60,000, which was conveyed to her husband, Frances' trustees were able to secure for her a settlement of £3,250 p.a. (the entire revenues of the Ingram estates at this time) as well as £1,000 'pin money' a year.[31] When she was eventually widowed she was able to reap all the revenues of the estates for her own use (by then they were producing £8,457 p.a.).[32]

By the early nineteenth century marriage contracts could involve enormous sums of money: Lady Hertford's marriage portion was £20,000 (with the expectation of further sums on her mother's death). For this she was to receive a jointure of £11,000, secured on her husband's estates in England and Ireland, as well as the continued use of Hertford House in London, and Temple Newsam during her lifetime.[33]

Children

It is often thought that the principal aim of aristocratic marriages was for the wife to provide at least one son, and hopefully more ('an heir and a spare'), to continue the dynasty and carry her husband's family name into the next generation. Isabella, with her nine sons, fulfilled this role abundantly and clearly wanted no more although her husband had other ideas when he wrote: 'I hope next weeke to get leve to come home and then we will get another boy for all you hope that you shall have no more'.[34]

While male heirs were obviously highly desirable, by the middle of the eighteenth century it was no longer a disaster if they did not materialise, provided suitable alternative arrangements could be made. Thus after Charles and Frances produced no sons their estates devolved to their eldest grandson, Hugo Charles Meynell, the eldest son of their third daughter Elizabeth, who then added the name Ingram to his own in order to perpetuate the family name.

Childlessness was likewise a misfortune but, as Ruth Larsen has shown,[35] not necessarily – from a dynastic perspective – a disaster. There is good reason for thinking that Henry seventh Viscount Irwin and his wife Anne made a deliberate choice not to have children on the grounds of their expense. Later, Emily Meynell Ingram's childlessness added greatly to her unhappiness as a widow, but in due course she took vicarious pleasure in the constant presence of the children of her youngest brother, Frederick, who made their home at Temple Newsam. On her death in 1904 she bequeathed to Frederick the Meynell family estates in Staffordshire and he changed his name appropriately. Similarly she bequeathed her Yorkshire estates including Temple Newsam, to her eldest nephew, the Hon. Edward Wood, who was later created Lord Irwin of the second creation.

Aristocratic women, and genteel women generally, were expected to take at least nominal charge of their daughters' education and upbringing. Once they were out of the nursery the girls would be provided with a governess, while the boys – until they went to boarding school – would be placed under the care of a tutor, often a cleric who doubled up as the household chaplain.

After her husband's death in 1702 (followed shortly by her father's) Isabella had no family or in-laws to whom she could turn for help to bring up her nine sons. Instead she leaned heavily on the estate steward 'honest John' Roades who stood *in loco parentis* for the boys as trustee and executor of their father's will. Between them, and with the help of the housekeeper Mildred Batchelor (and no doubt Nanny Backhouse), they saw to their early upbringing, sending them to the Revd William Herbert's school in Normanton and later to William Thomlinson's school in York. The eldest two went to Eton and Christ's College, Cambridge.

Evidently the boys were never easy to manage, the eldest in particular having inherited their father's love of sport and good living, not to mention a tendency to sloth. Their education probably suffered since they were so often in the company of the estate servants. Thus four of them were dispatched to the Continent, either for a Grand Tour (Edward and Rich), or for additional education (Henry and William). The story of her eldest son Edward is well known.[36] His main contribution to Temple Newsam being his purchase of 'about 40' paintings by Antonio Marini (of which eighteen are still in the house), paid for by Isabella 'sight unseen' back in England.[37]

In contrast to the robust education of Isabella's boys, Frances' five girls (fig. 2) were given a very sheltered early life, spent entirely at home. Their governess was probably a Miss Scott who appears to have remained with the family for over forty years, eventually becoming Frances' companion.[38] She was almost certainly joined by specialist tutors for drawing, dancing, and French from time to time. Later the girls were taken to London and Bath to introduce them into wider society and prepare them for marriage.[39] The good education of the eldest daughter, the future Lady Hertford, was commented upon by outsiders and was an obvious recommendation for her in the marriage market.[40]

FIGURE 2

The Five Daughters of Charles 9th Viscount Irwin, by Benjamin Wilson, oil on canvas.

HALIFAX COLLECTION
(ON LOAN TO TEMPLE NEWSAM HOUSE)

The household

Lady Irwin my wife desires that ye ducks and wild turkeys be well propagated for she proposes a visit next year … she desires you'll take great care with ye linen, china etc.
Henry seventh Viscount Irwin to his steward Robert Hopkinson, 1736.[41]

A fundamental belief of the landed aristocracy in the eighteenth and nineteenth centuries, among women as well as men, was that their inherited estates were held 'in trust' for the next generation, and it was their responsibility to pass them on in a better condition. While their husbands were still alive their wives had the care of the household as their main semi-public function. This included the supervision of servants and of the education of the younger children, and the provision of basic medical care. In addition to their 'drawing room' accomplishments (needlework, music, writing, etc.) it was considered a great asset to have some additional practical skill in the domestic sphere. Taking a close and knowledgeable interest in the proceedings of the dairy, the stillroom, the apothecary store, or even the kitchen and laundry, was greatly esteemed.[42] It was the wife's responsibility to enter up the housekeeping books, or at least to inspect and approve them regularly. There is clear evidence that Isabella, Anne (wife of Henry, seventh Viscount) and Frances conformed to these expectations. In the more sophisticated world of the nineteenth century, Lady Hertford, Lady William Gordon and Mrs Meynell Ingram frequently delegated these responsibilities to the higher servants.

When they became widowed, their roles often became much more complex. They may have been appointed a trustee or executor, as Isabella became for her husband and for at least two of her sons, or inherited the estates outright, as Frances and Emily did. Isabella had the support of her steward John Roades who kept meticulous accounts.[43] But she also had the enormous problem of honouring her late husband's legacies, which, after the losses of the South Sea Bubble, ultimately required a private Act of Parliament to enable a mortgage of £20,000 to be taken out over the property for the necessary funds to be raised.

Frances greatly enjoyed her role as chatelaine (describing herself – aged twenty-nine – as 'a downright old fashioned country gentlewoman')[44] as all her letters and account books testify.[45] In the nineteenth century Emily took a more detached view. She let go the Leather family who had almost become hereditary stewards of the estates and took on a young professional land agent instead, Mr John Farrer. With her encouragement he completely re-organised the management of the estates in the late 1880s and with great effect.[46] When she had inherited in 1871 her properties were valued for probate at £180,000 and her income was assessed at £45,000 p.a. in 1879.[47] However when she died in 1904, despite the slump in agricultural rents and because of a more flexible approach to mines, forestry and real estate development, together with investments in stocks and shares, her real and personal estates were valued at nearly £2,250,000.[48] Her income from investments alone exceeded £167,000 p.a. by this date.[49]

Inside the house the supervision of the indoor servants, especially the female domestic staff, was considered a major responsibility of the lady of the house in the eighteenth century (fig. 3). Male servants, especially those concerned with the stables or gardens, were generally the responsibility of the man of the house, or, in his absence, the estate or house steward.

It is not possible to consider the role of servants at Temple Newsam at any length in the short scope of this study, but their numbers varied according to the needs of the family. A snapshot in 1758, at a time when there were no children in the house, revealed eleven female and seventeen male servants.[50] Their combined annual wages bill was £233-10s-0d (out of the total running costs of the household of £2,175).

Accomplishments

Beyond the everyday running of their houses aristocratic women would be concerned to make use of and develop their personal artistic accomplishments. Their education equipped them not only for their role as wives, mothers and social networkers, but also for their many hours spent in elegant but useful leisure: needlework, drawing (especially embroidery patterns, later portraits and landscapes etc. in watercolour), playing music or singing. Foreign languages – especially French – an ability to write good letters and read well out loud to the family circle were all highly esteemed. More adventurous pastimes such as scrolled paper work, woodturning, or shell work were certainly admired and encouraged for their decorative and useful qualities. Advanced intellectual or eccentric accomplishments however, such as published literary authorship, were only rarely found among women of the aristocracy until much later.

Most women of the Ingram family possessed at least one of these classic accomplishments, if not more. Isabella had a well-stocked library at her house in

Windsor, much of which later came to Temple Newsam.[51] Hers and Frances' letters have a similar spontaneous liveliness about them, often full of witty and revealing asides. They were clearly intended to be read aloud to friends. Lady Anne Howard not only wrote poetry but also amusing and entertaining letters to her relatives.[52]

The Scarburgh sisters (Anne and Elizabeth, wives of the seventh Viscount and his brother Charles, and Henrietta Jenkinson) almost certainly had a hand in the needlework suite of the new Picture Gallery or its carpet (fig. 4); their nieces in Sussex were certainly frequently hard at work on chairs and carpets.[53] A revealing glimpse is given in one of their letters:

> *I am a great work woman for I am doing a Triming for a Negligee… Lady Irwin works very hard at her Carpet every morning, Miss Bell at her Chair & my Cousin at her Handkerchief which my sister drew for her…*[54]

Similarly, both Frances and her daughters were often to be found drawing patterns for and embroidering bed hangings or personalised handkerchiefs for their friends.[55]

In music there is plenty of evidence that both the men and the women of the family had well-developed tastes: the accounts recall the arrival of new and up to date musical instruments throughout the eighteenth century.[56] In the later nineteenth century Mrs Meynell Ingram became a major patron of the Leeds Musical Festival.[57] Her highly developed visual sense can be seen in her fine watercolours, and later in her 'painterly' approach to architecture and decoration.[58]

FIGURE 4

Sofa, upholstered in needlework dated 27 September 1743 and 17 December 1748, probably part of the original carpet border made for the Picture Gallery at Temple Newsam.

LADY LEVER ART GALLERY, NATIONAL MUSEUMS ON MERSEYSIDE

Patronage in the house and park

The arrival of a new bride at a country house often coincided with new decorating and furnishing activity. With her mother-in-law finally departed to Windsor in 1718 the new Lady Irwin, Lady Anne Howard, was treated to a mass of new furniture and decorations including a splendid new state bed.[59] Later in the century, anticipating her move north, Frances ordered great quantities of new plate on her own account, and proceeded to decorate her first bedroom in the house with a 'pillar and arch' paper, and at the same time softening her predecessor's heavy Palladian plasterwork with rococo flourishes.[60]

Isabella's earlier reign at Temple Newsam was not characterised by extensive new decorations or furnishings possibly because the short-lived second Viscount Irwin had done much immediately before her arrival.[61] At Windsor and at Horsham, however, she continued to buy new furniture and silver, periodically redecorating her rooms in the fashions of the day.[62] She was also called upon to advise her bachelor sons, especially for Arthur's new house in Grosvenor Square in 1735, [63] and for George in 1743.[64]

Splendid furniture poured into Temple Newsam in the late eighteenth century from the workshops of Chippendale the elder and younger, and John Linnell, among others.[65] Other works of art arrived via the art market: Rubens' *Holy*

Family with St John the Baptist, the Claude *Pastoral Landscape*, Titian's *Young Man*.[66] The project to modernise the south wing, having begun as a joint venture with her husband (with Robert Adam, 'Capability' Brown and John Carr providing advice) was left to Frances to complete.[67] She chose the local architect William Johnson, possibly because he was near at hand. The inventory compiled after her death in 1807 showed that the house combined luxury and comfort, together with the modern and the old-fashioned.[68]

The three women owners of Temple Newsam in the nineteenth century, Lady Hertford, Lady William Gordon and Mrs Meynell Ingram, were all women of great taste and discrimination.[69] Lady Hertford and Mrs Meynell Ingram were both distinguished collectors with an eclectic eye, and both made improvements to the house that generally respected the taste of past owners. Many of Lady Hertford's decorative schemes of the late 1820s (in the Chinese Room, the Great Hall, the Crimson Bed and Dressing rooms)[70] have now been restored, as have Mrs Meynell Ingram's of the 1880s (principally in the west wing).[71]

Of all the women who have lived at Temple Newsam, Frances was probably the one most deeply smitten by the place, almost certainly from as early as her first visit in 1756 as the fiancée of Charles, the future ninth Viscount. She took to country life with relish, and within a few years proudly described herself to her smart London friends as 'an old fashioned country gentlewoman in an old worn out house with my four girls'.[72]

Within ten years of her marriage to Charles work had started on a new naturalistic park under 'Capability' Brown (which she called 'Brownifications'), although care was taken to retain the old-fashioned baroque East Avenue of the previous generation. An early feature was a gravel walk for Frances' exercise ('always a resource & much made use of'), and as time advanced she and her husband took great pleasure in the general progress.[73] Even though the weather and Mr Brown might put them in 'a woful dirty pickle' it fitted her ideal of life of 'bright days, serene air and merry children'.[74] Her participation is vividly described in 1767:

> *I have not only been out [in the wet fog] but actually stood still while Col Pitt & my husband have been Brownifying my dear gravel walk, his little wife carried stakes for them to mark out places for shrubs & I stood by to give my approbation.*[75]

Her hands-on approach was absolutely genuine for three years later she wrote: 'I am out almost the whole day tho' it has been dreadfully cold, but I have taken it into my head to plant this spring & I never feel cold upon these occasions'.[76]

She saw her landscape as a metaphor for the good life, comparing it to an idealised landscape painting:

> *I apply myself to my beauteous Claude where the scene always enchants me; the trees are green, the waters placid & serene & the air has a warmth very comfortable. Altogether it is just as one's mind should be; no boundless passions or turbulent ambition to perturb one's breast but the stream of life to flow peacefully & unruffled,*

sometimes through flowery meads & sometimes through brake till at length it reaches the ocean of eternity.[77]

The outer world: politics, piety, philanthropy.

… my little Horsham business went on flourishingly …
Frances Viscountess Irwin to Susan Countess Gower, 1780.[78]

Frances' 'little Horsham business' was the management of the two parliamentary seats at Horsham, the family's pocket borough. It had been acquired as part of the inheritance of Isabella whose family owned the estate at Hills Place nearby, and which remained the family's secondary seat.[79] The very few burgesses (voters) of the town were almost all 'in the pocket' of the Ingrams who were therefore able to send any candidate of their choice to Parliament. It remained in their hands until 1811 when it was sold to the Duke of Norfolk for over £90,000.[80] In Leeds there was no worthwhile political interest since the town did not return its own MPs until after the Great Reform Act of 1832.

Isabella, naturally, took a close interest in the affairs of Horsham, especially during her widowhood when she lived in Windsor but spent long periods visiting her younger sons there. When the family bought out the remaining political interest of a neighbouring family in 1723 she contributed £1,000 from her own funds.[81] The family's instincts were Whig but they played no major part in government: the real usefulness of a seat in the House of Commons was its proximity to power and lucrative sinecures. It was all the more necessary since the Irwin title was a Scottish one, which did not entitle them to sit in the House of Lords in London.[82] Thus three of Isabella's sons sat as the town's MP, as well as her grandson Charles before he succeeded to the viscountcy.[83]

Frances took no great interest in politics until her widowhood. In 1780 she became incensed at the revolt of Rockingham and the Yorkshire Association against the King and Lord North, and became a committed Tory.[84] Horsham became known as 'Lady Irwin's seat' and was put at the disposal of Pitt and the government. Lord William Gordon managed it on her behalf: the price for any suitable candidate was £4,000 per parliament. She managed to fend off the encroachments of the Duke of Norfolk whose candidates contested the election in 1790 and 1806, but whose early successes were lost on appeal.[85] Her daughter

FIGURE 6

Mrs Meynell Ingram outside the Orphanage at Hoar Cross, photograph c.1890.

LEEDS MUSEUMS AND GALLERIES, TEMPLE NEWSAM HOUSE

Lady Hertford was a passionate Tory and she used her influence with the Prince Regent to great effect in 1812 in dissuading him from inviting the Whigs to form a government.[86] She was mercilessly satirised in the opposition press (fig. 5).

Despite being the daughter of a Whig cabinet minister, the granddaughter of a Prime Minister, and the wife of a Tory MP, Emily Meynell Ingram was never seriously active in party politics, least of all after becoming a widow. Possibly because of her dislike of Gladstone, she eventually became an active Tory and in 1903 hosted Joseph Chamberlain at the time of an important political rally in Leeds.

During the eighteenth century the Ingram family appear to have been orthodox subscribers to mainstream Anglicanism. They generally included a chaplain as a member of the household, who was sometimes the tutor to the children and the incumbent of Whitkirk. Isabella's enquiring mind also embraced religious thought and her library at Windsor included a large number of devotional and theological books. She may have considered Roman Catholicism, as an unusual manuscript testifies.[87] Frances' religious convictions are not known, but soon after she was married her trustee wrote, perhaps in jest '... if I hear your building a church, erecting almshouses, charity schools etc. I shall not be surprised'.[88] However, she abolished the domestic chapel in the house in her alterations of the 1790s, giving the pulpit to the Methodist chapel in Halton. She was not sympathetic to her gardener when he converted to Methodism, though, as she considered this interfered with his work.[89]

The family were generous subscribers to local charitable institutions and the parish church during the eighteenth century. Frances was particularly good at sponsoring the education of poor children in the neighbourhood, enabling boys to find apprenticeships and girls to work as seamstresses.[90] Her daughter Lady William Gordon was remembered locally until the end of the nineteenth century for her acts of charity and left a trust for the local poor to be administered by the vicar of Whitkirk.[91]

Mrs Meynell Ingram's piety was of a different order. She wholeheartedly embraced the Anglo-Catholic movement of which her brother was a leading light. She took great consolation in her faith during her early widowhood in particular, and commissioned the church of the Holy Angels, just outside the park at Hoar Cross, from G. F. Bodley and Thomas Garner, as a memorial to her husband. It is often described as one of the most moving of all Victorian churches. She took the closest interest in its construction and decoration and it remains the expression of her personal spirituality.[92] Her patron saint was St Vincent de Paul whose statue was placed in the chapel of All Souls. He advocated a combination of social responsibility and personal devotion which resulted in Emily's founding an orphanage at Hoar Cross and many other acts of charity (fig. 6).[93] She also built and re-ordered several churches, and endowed a number of charitable and theological institutions.[94]

Sport and 'play'

Much of country house life revolved around the sporting activities of the men, which was also where much political activity took place. At Temple Newsam shooting was the favourite diversion of many generations of the Ingram family, although they were also entertained by hunting, horse racing, and cock fighting at different times.

None of these activities was enjoyed by the women of the family, even as spectators. Although she was a great believer in moderate exercise and fresh air, and in hunting and shooting for men, Frances was disappointed that her husband Charles left for a shooting party 'on the moors' so soon after their honeymoon.[95] Her sister-in-law also satirised Lady Rockingham's overdressed appearance when following her husband on a shoot at Wentworth Woodhouse in 1749.[96] Riding, on the other hand, was an esteemed pastime for aristocratic women: Laura Meynell Ingram, one of Emily's sisters-in-law, was considered one of the finest horsewomen in England before her death in 1870. There were of course dangers: Emily is said to have had a miscarriage,[97] and Hugo Francis died from complications following a riding accident.

Women were more often entertained by indoor sport, or 'play', namely cards and gambling. Isabella was partial to it, noting her small losses in her account books. Frances on the other hand was strongly against it, not because she was a prig but perhaps because it represented all that she disliked about sophisticated metropolitan life.[98] Yet, so ingrained was gambling as part of aristocratic life, that even she was obliged to frequent the tables in grand London houses while chaperoning her debutante daughters during the Season.[99]

However, the most stylish and enthusiastic sportswoman of the family was Emily Meynell Ingram. For eleven years from 1886 she was the proud owner of the 360 ton yacht the *Ariadne*, with its full-time crew of about thirty (fig. 1). Generally twice a year she and a group of friends would spend up to two or three months cruising in the Mediterranean in the early spring, and in Scandinavia or the Baltic in the summer. They recorded their journeys with witty poems, watercolours and artistic photographs in the Log Books that reveal an unexpectedly informal aspect of Victorian life.

Thus the story of Temple Newsam is inextricably linked to the story of its women. Many other characters or different facets of their lives could have been considered, and from different periods, but it is hoped that enough is suggested here to provoke the admiration and sympathy of present day visitors to their 'ancient Dwelling'.[100]

I am particularly grateful to the following who have shown me their unpublished research on various aspects this subject: Dr Ruth Larsen, Julie Day, Michael Hall, Melissa Gallimore, Lucy Wood and Dr David Connell.

1   PRO, Granville MSS, 30/29/4/2, Letter from Frances Viscountess Irwin to Susan Countess Gower, 8 August 1779.

2   See for example West Yorkshire Archive Service, Sheepscar (WYAS), Temple Newsam MSS (TN), EA 3/26, 'A Catalogue of all the Household Furniture, Plate, Linen & China etc of the Rt Hon Lady Dowager Irwin (Deceased) at her late Dwelling-House at Windsor… which will be sold by Auction… 11 of October 1764'.

3   The great majority of her surviving papers are to be found in WYAS, TN/C/7-18 (passim) (correspondence); TN/EA/14 et seq (account books etc). Transcripts of some of her correspondence are found in WYAS, Pawson MSS, Acc 1038, Letter Books 4-10. Other documents are found at Horsham Museum, Machell Ingram MSS.

4   See Albery, W., *A Parliamentary History of Horsham 1295-1885* (London, 1927); also Hughes, A. F. and J. Knight, *Hills: Horsham's Lost Stately Home and Garden* (exhibition catalogue) (Horsham Museum Society 1999), p. 24.

5   For example she annotated a conciliatory letter dated 13 December 1718 from her son's steward Robert Hopkinson who suggested an amiable resolution of a conflict between mother and son with the sarcastic comment 'Friendly advice to give up my Inst writ to an ungrateful son wholly governed by ye proud family of ye Howards who never served any body but for their own interest'; WYAS, TN/C/12/27.

6   The Marriage Settlement deed is exhibited in the exhibition. WYAS, TN/F/17/50.

7   A good account of the Frances' problems is given in Budge, Adrian, 'Temple Newsam and 'the Good Shepheards'', *Leeds Arts Calendar* 98 (1986), pp. 8-15.

8   PRO/30/29/4/2, Letters of Viscountess Irwin to Lady Susan Stewart, passim.

9   Frances' documents are to be found at WYAS, TN/C/18-19 passim (correspondence); TN/EA/14,15,16 (household accounts etc); Pawson MSS, Acc 1038, Letter Books 4-10 passim.

10   See Connell, D., 'The collection of paintings made by the Ingram Family of Temple Newsam from the seventeenth to the nineteenth century' (PhD Thesis, University of Leeds, 1992).

11   Albery, *Parliamentary History*, passim.

12   The main group of documents concerning Emily Meynell Ingram are to be found at the Borthwick Institute, University of York, Halifax MSS, A7, Seven Diaries 1854-1903; A2, 267 Correspondence; at the Staffordshire County Archive Service, Stafford, Meynell MSS, D861/P/3/6 Vols. 33-34, Francis Meynell's 'Commentaries on Mrs Meynell Ingram's Diaries' and his 'Recollections…'; D861/P/1/17, Correspondence; D861/P/2/1, private account books; D861/E/2/2-6, Estate Account Books & Ledgers; D861/E/8, Building Accounts etc for Church of Holy Angels, Hoar Cross; and at WYAS, Meynell Ingram Estates, Acc No 4317, for miscellaneous estate documents. For her early life in particular see Lockhart, J.G., *Charles Lindley Viscount Halifax* (London, 1935), part 1, passim.

13   The reasons for her childlessness are not known but see Hall, M., 'Emily Meynell Ingram and Holy Angels, Hoar Cross, Staffordshire: A Study in Patronage', forthcoming article in *Architectural History* (2004). I am grateful to Michael Hall for letting me see the draft of his article before it went to press.

14   See Meynell, Lady Mary, *Sunshine and Shadow over a Long Life* (London, 1933) passim and esp. pp. 185-203.

15   See Hall, M., 'Emily Meynell Ingram and Hoar Cross: Women and Anglo-Catholic Church Patronage', unpublished paper given to the Victorian Society Symposium, *Women and Architecture in the*

nineteenth century, November 1996, and Hall, 'Emily Meynell Ingram and Holy Angels'.

16 Connell, 'The Collection of Paintings', passim; and Connell, D., 'A Victorian Art Lover, the Hon Mrs Meynell Ingram', *Leeds Arts Calendar* 106 (1990), pp. 17-27.

17 Gilbert, G., 'The Victorian Chapel at Temple Newsam', *Leeds Arts Calendar* 62 (1966), pp. 5-9, and Gilbert, G., 'A Last Look at the Victorian Chapel', *Leeds Arts Calendar* 76 (1975), pp. 18-20.

18 Gilbert, G., 'C E Kempe's Staircase and Interiors at Temple Newsam 1894', *Leeds Arts Calendar* 65 (1969), pp. 6-11.

19 Wells-Cole, A., 'The Dining Room at Temple Newsam', *Leeds Arts Calendar* 110 (1992), pp. 16-24.

20 Horsham Museum, Machell Ingram MSS, 792.1.

21 Budge, A., 'The Good Shepheards', passim; for example WYAS, Pawson MSS, Acc 1038, Letter Book 7, B6 B23/119, Letter from John Waple to Frances Shepheard, 11 June 1756.

22 Meynell, Lady Mary, *Sunshine and Shadows*, pp. 145-147.

23 PRO/30/29/4/2, Letter from Frances Viscountess Irwin to Susan Countess Gower (no 52), n.d., c. 1780.

24 Bulloch, J.M., *The House of Gordon* (Aberdeen, 1903), p. 392.

25 Arthur's surviving letters to Isabella usually begin 'My Pretty Dear penny'. WYAS, TN/C/7; Borthwick Institute, Halifax MSS, A2.267.14.

26 Borthwick Institute, Halifax MSS, A2.125, Letter of the Hon Charles Wood to his wife, 4 June 1872.

27 Castle Howard, Carlisle MSS, J8/1/127-128,175 Letters of Lady Mary Howard to the Earl of Carlisle, 13, 23 & 28 April 1721. Cited by Larsen R. M., 'Dynastic Domesticity: the role of elite women in the Yorkshire country house 1685-1858', (PhD Thesis, University of York, 2003), pp. 249-250.

28 WYAS, TN/C/13/37, Letter from Robert Hopkinson to Isabella Viscountess Irwin, 27 June 1723.

29 WYAS, TN/C/13/135 Letter from Henry Viscount Irwin to Robert Hopkinson, 7 November 1738.

30 WYAS, Pawson MSS, Acc 1038, Letter Book 7, B6 B23a/188 Proposals for a settlement.

31 WYAS, Pawson MSS, Acc 1038, Letter Book 7, B6 B23/9 Letter of Charles Waple to Mrs Charles Ingram 26 October 1758.

32 From uncatalogued documents given to WYAS, by Lord Halifax 1995, Estate Accounts for 1778.

33 WYAS, TN/F/17/50, Marriage Settlement of the Hon Isabella Shepheard Ingram, 1776.

34 WYAS, TN/C/7, Letter from Arthur third Viscount Irwin to Isabella Viscountess Irwin 23 February [1700?].

35 Larsen, 'Dynastic Domesticity', pp. 150-1.

36 Gilbert, C., 'A Nobleman and the Grand Tour: Lord Irwin and Marco Ricci', *Apollo*, lxxxiii, May 1966, pp. 358-63.

37 Connell, 'The Collection of Paintings', passim.

38 Miss Scott was first mentioned in Isabella's correspondence with Susan Countess Gower on 5 June 1768 (PRO, Glanville MSS, 30/29/4/2); on 8 May 1799 she drove with Frances to Wood Hall, near Wetherby for dinner (WYAS, TN/EA 14/16); on the eve of the Prince of Wales' visit 1806 she was described by Lady Hertford as 'putting her best gown in order that she might look to advantage' (British Library, Hertford Papers, Egerton MSS, 3260, ff. 159-162).

39 For example Frances wrote to Susan Countess Gower from Bath 28 October 1770 'Ld I has sent me to two balls to show the children what they were. Bell was delighted with the first but grew rather tired at the second' (PRO/30/29/4/2).

40 'Her education has been such as to give us great hopes of her turning out to be what we would wish his wife to be'. Lewis, W. S. (ed.), *Horace Walpole's Correspondence* (New Haven, 1937-83, 48 vols), xxxix, 265 (Lady Isabella Fitzroy, Marchioness of Hertford to Horace Walpole 25 September 1775).

41 WYAS, TN/C/15/32, Letter from Henry seventh Viscount Irwin to his steward Robert Hopkinson, 19 June 1736.

42 Isabella's library included volumes on domestic science (e.g. Richard Bradley's *The Country Housewife and Lady's Director* (1736) and medicine (e.g. Thomas Short's *Medicina Britannica* (1747), WYAS, TN/EA/3/36, Catalogue.

43 For example WYAS, TN/EA/13/54, Jo: Roades account book of disbursements for and on account of Edward fourth Viscount Irwin, 1702-1708.

44 PRO/30/29/4/2, Undated letter to Lady Susan Stewart, c. 1763.

45 Her surviving housekeeping account books include those for 1758-1764. (TN/EA/14/13) and 1796-1804 (TN/EA/14/17). Her surviving household account books are those for 1786-1796 (TN/EA/14/15) and 1797-1800 (TN/EA/14/16).

46 See Staffordshire Archive Service, Stafford, Meynell MSS, D861/E/2/2-6, 'The Hon Mrs Meynell Ingram's Yorkshire Estates Summary of Accounts' series 1892-1897.

47 WYAS, Meynell Ingram Estates, Acc 4317, Probate records 5/1; see Bateman, J., *The Great Landowners of Great Britain and Ireland* (London, 1879), p. 231.

48 WYAS, Meynell Ingram Estates, Acc 4162, Probate records 8.

49 ibid.

50 WYAS, Pawson MSS, Letter Book 7 (flyleaf). The list itemises the servants with their annual wages. It also revealed 'To Lady Irwin for housekeeping £600'.

51 WYAS, TN/EA/3/26, Catalogue.

52 For example her letters to her brother-in-law Charles Ingram December-March 1718-1719 WYAS, Pawson MSS, Acc 1038, Letter Book 6 B6 B20/352,353,354.

53 See Exhibition Guide with entry relating to the needlework settee lent by the Lady Lever Art Gallery; information kindly given by Lucy Wood.

54 Horsham Museum, Machell Ingram MSS, 794.6 Letter from Elizabeth Ingram to Frances Ingram 7 November 1758.

55 Borthwick Institute Halifax MSS, A5.3.2 'Catalogue of china, old chairs etc…' p. 13. For example PRO/30/29/4/2, Letters from Frances Viscountess Irwin to Lady Susan Stewart (later Susan Countess Gower and later Susan Marchioness of Stafford) 8 September 1765, 7 October 1765, 2 February 1766 and 13 August 1770.

56 See the Temple Newsam house inventories of 1714, 1721, 1734, 1736, 1740 WYAS, TN/EA/3/14-21 passim, and of 1808, Yorkshire Archaeological Society DD54.

57 Meynell, Lady Mary, *Sunshine and Shadow*, p. 68. For another view see Spark F., and J. Bennett, *Leeds Musical Festivals 1858-1889* (1892) p. 241.

58 Hall, M., 'Emily Meynell Ingram and Holy Angels', forthcoming article for *Architectural History* (2004).

59 Gilbert, C., 'The Temple Newsam Furniture Bills', *Furniture History* 3 (1967), p. 20; Wells Cole, A., 'The Great Hall at Temple Newsam', *Leeds Arts Calendar* 106 (1990), p. 5; WYAS, TN/EA/12/6.

60 WYAS, TN/C/23/71 Letter from John Murray to Frances Ingram, 24 August 1758; Lomax, J., 'The Grandeur of Plate', *Leeds Arts Calendar* 107 (1990), p. 23.

61 Wells-Cole, A., 'The Great Hall', p. 5.

62 Lomax, 'The Grandeur', pp. 11-12.

63 WYAS, Pawson MSS, Acc 1038, Letter Book 6, B6, B14/217, Letter from Arthur sixth Viscount Irwin to William Ingram, 26 August 1735.

64 WYAS, TN/C/16, no number c.23, Letter from George Ingram to Isabella Viscountess Irwin, 21 May 1743.

65 Gilbert, 'The Temple Newsam Furniture Bills', passim; WYAS, TN/EA/12/5.

66 Connell, 'The Collection of Paintings', passim.

67 PRO/30/29/4/2, Letter from Frances Viscountess Irwin to Susan Marchioness of Stafford, 14 June 1795.

68 Yorkshire Archaeological Society, DD54, published as 'The Temple Newsam Inventory 1808', *Leeds Arts Calendar* 100 (1987) pp. 3-49.

69 See for example Connell, 'A Victorian Art Lover', pp. 17-27; Borthwick Institute, Halifax MSS, A5.3.2, 'Catalogue of china, old furniture etc 1880'; Wallace Collection archives, 'Inventory of all the Superb Furniture, Glasses, China, Pictures and Effects at Hertford House Manchester Square May 1834'; Savill, R., *The Wallace Collection Catalogue of Sevres Porcelain* (London, 1988), passim.

70 Wells-Cole, A., 'Another Look at Lady Hertford's Chinese Drawing Room', *Leeds Arts Calendar* 98 (1986), pp. 16-22; Wells-Cole, A., 'The Great Hall at Temple Newsam', *Leeds Arts Calendar*, 106 (1990), pp. 3-16.

71 Wells-Cole, A., 'Some Bedrooms and Dressing Rooms of the West Wing', *Leeds Arts Calendar* 112(1993), pp. 7-28.

72 PRO/30/29/4/2, Letter from Frances Viscountess Irwin to Lady Susan Stewart, n.d., c. 1763.

73 PRO/30/29/4/2, Letter from Frances Viscountess Irwin to Lady Susan Stewart, 8 April 1766.

74 ibid.

75 PRO/30/29/4/2, Letter from Frances Viscountess Irwin to Lady Susan Stewart, 5 Febarury 1767.

76 PRO/30/29/4/2, Letter from Frances Viscountess Irwin to Lady Susan Stewart, 2 March 1770.

77 PRO/30/29/4/2, Letter from Frances Viscountess Irwin to Lady Susan Stewart, 14 December 1766.

78 PRO/30/29/4/2, Letter from Frances Viscountess Irwin to Lady Susan Stewart, Undated letter c. 1780.

79 Henning, R. D., *History of Parliament: the Commons 1660-1690* (London, 1983), iii, p. 1.

80 Albery, W., *Parliamentary History*, chs VI-X passim; Thorne, R.G., *The House of Commons 1790-1820* (London, 1986), i, pp. 394-395.

81 Hughes and Knight, *Hills*, passim.

82 Charles and Frances lobbied unsuccessfully to obtain a peerage of the United Kingdom (PRO/30/29/4/2, Letters from Frances Viscountess Irwin to Lady Susan Stewart, 10 February 1761 and 2 May 1763). Charles was elected one of the sixteen representative Scottish peers in 1768; Jones, C., and D. Lewis Jones (eds.), *Peers, Politics and Power: the House of Lords 1603-1911* (London, 1986), p. 274.

83 Albery, *Parliamentary History*, passim and pp. 501-502; Sedgwick, R., *The House of Commons 1715-1754* (London, 1970), ii, pp. 166-168.

84 PRO/30/29/4/2 Letter from Frances Viscountess Irwin to Susan Countess Gower, 21 January 1780.

85 Thorne, *The House of Commons*, pp. 394-395; Albery, passim.

86 The literature on Lady Hertford is enormous. See for references Budge, A., 'Lady Hertford, a Quean of the Regency?', *Leeds Arts Calendar* 86 (1980) pp. 11-19.

87 WYAS, TN/C/10, Apologetic for the Roman Catholick faith, 16 June 1713.

88 WYAS, Pawson MSS, Letter Book 6, B6 B23/9, Letter from John Waple to Frances Ingram 26 October 1758.

89 PRO/30/29/4/2, Letter of 13 August 1770.

90 WYAS, TN/EA 12/20, Charities etc.

91 Platt, G.M. and J. W. Morkill, *Records of the Parish of Whitkirk*, (Leeds, 1892), p. 48.

92 Hall, 'Emily Meynell Ingram and Holy Angels'.

93 ibid.

94 WYAS, Meynell Ingram MSS, Acc 4162.8, Probate documents.

95 WYAS, Pawson MSS, Letter Book 6, B6 B23/103, Letter from Anne Viscountess Irwin to Frances Ingram, 24 August 1758.

96 'Her clothes are white satin embroidered with silver & colours and all over vastly fine'. WYAS, Pawson MSS, Letter Book 6, B6 B20/236, Letter from Isabella Irwin to her grandmother Isabella Viscountess Irwin, 1 July 1749.

97 Hall, 'Emily Meynell Ingram and Holy Angels'.

98 WYAS, Pawson MSS, Acc 1038, Letter Book 6, B6 B23/124, Letter from John Waple to Frances Ingram, 26 April 1759.

99 'My life passes voyaging from one gaming table to another ...' PRO/30/29/4/2/45, Undated letter from Frances Viscountess Irwin to Susan Countess Gower, c. 1776.

100 PRO/30/29/4/2, As described by Frances Viscountess Irwin to Susan Countess Gower, 8 August 1774.

FURTHER READING

In addition to the guidebooks published by each of the houses, the following titles are suggested for further reading.

Adams, S. and S., *The Complete Servant*, Lewes 1989.

Baird, R., *Mistress of the House: Great Ladies and Grand Houses 1670-1830*, London, 2003.

Bamfield, V., *On the Strength: The Story of the British Army Wife*, London, 1974.

Mrs Beeton, *Book of Household Management*, London, 1861.

Bermingham, A., *Learning to Draw, Studies in the Cultural History of a Polite and Useful Art*, New Haven, 2000.

Budge, A., 'Lady Hertford, a Quean of the Regency?', *Leeds Arts Calendar* 86 (1980).

Budge, A., 'Temple Newsam and 'the Good Shepherds', *Leeds Arts Calendar* 98 (1986).

Christie, C., *The British Country House in the Eighteenth Century*, Manchester, 2000.

Davidoff, L., *The Best Circles. Society, Etiquette and the Season*, London, 1973.

Dolan, B., *Ladies of the Grand Tour*, London, 2001.

Flanders, J., *The Victorian House: Domestic Life from Childbirth to Deathbed*, London, 2003.

Foreman, A., *Georgiana's World. The Illustrated Georgiana, Duchess of Devonshire*, London, 2001.

Gerard, J., *Country House Life, Family and Servants, 1815-1914*, Oxford, 1994.

Gilbert, C., *Furniture at Temple Newsam House and Lotherton Hall*, Leeds and London, 1978.

Girouard, M., *The Victorian Country House*, New Haven, 1985.

Gleadle, K., and S. Richardson (eds.), *Women in British Politics, 1760-1860: The Power of the Petticoat*, London, 2000.

Guest, H., *Small Change. Women, Learning, Patriotism, 1750-1810*, Chicago, 2000.

Hall, I. and E. Hall. *Burton Constable. A Century of Patronage.* Beverley, 1991.

Hardyment, C., *Home Comfort. A History of Domestic Arrangements*, London, 1992.

Hickman, K., *Daughters of Britannia: The Lives and Times of Diplomatic Wives*, London, 1999.

Hill, B., *Servants, English Servants in the Eighteenth Century*, Oxford, 1996.

Holmes, R., *Redcoat: The British Soldier in the Age of Horse and Musket*, London, 2002.

Horn, P., *The Rise and Fall of the Victorian Servant*, Dublin, 1975.

Horn, P., *Ladies of the Manor: Wives and Daughter in Country-house Society, 1830-1918*, Stroud, 1991.

Jalland, P., *Women, Marriage and Politics, 1860-1914*, Oxford, 1986.

Lewis, J.S., *In the Family Way. Childbearing in the British Aristocracy 1760-1860*, New Brunswick, 1986.

Lewis, J.S., *Sacred to Female Patriotism*, London, 2003.

Lomax, J., *British Silver at Temple Newsam and Lotherton Hall*, Leeds, 1992.

Lummis, T., and J. Marsh, *The Woman's Domain: Women and the English Country House*, London, 1993.

Mauchline, M., *Harewood House. One of the Treasure Houses of Britain*, Second Edition, Ashbourne, 1992.

Mendelson, S.H., and P. Crawford, *Women in Early Modern England, 1550-1720*, Oxford, 1998.

Murray, M., *Castle Howard: the Life and Times of A Stately Home*, York, 1994.

Perkin, J., *Women and Marriage in Nineteenth-Century England*, London, 1989.

Reynolds, K.D., *Aristocratic Women and Political Society in Victorian Britain*, Oxford, 1998.

Sambrook, P., *The Country House Servant, Stroud*, 1999.

Sambrook, P. and P. Brears, *The Country House Kitchen, 1650-1900*, Stroud, 1996.

Saumarez Smith, C., *Eighteenth-Century Decoration. Design and the Domestic Interior in England*, London, 1993.

Sloan, K., *A Noble Art, Amateur Artists and Drawing Masters, c.1600-1800*, London, 2000.

Stone, L., *Family, Sex and Marriage in England 1500-1800*, London, 1977.

Thompson, F. M. L., *English Society in the Nineteenth Century*, London, 1963.

Vickery, A., *The Gentleman's Daughter. Women's Lives in Georgian England*, London, 1998.

Vickery, A. (ed.), *Women, Privilege, and Power: British Politics, 1750 to the Present*, Stanford, 2001.

Waterfield, G. et al. *Below Stairs, 400 Years of Servants' Portraits*, London, 2003.

Waterson, M., *The Servants' Hall, A Domestic History*, London, 1980.

Wilson, C.A., *The Country House Kitchen Garden, 1600-1950*, Stroud, 1900.

Wilson, R. and A. Mackley, *Creating Paradise: The Building of the English Country House, 1660-1880*, London, 2000.